PRAISE FOR

FIRST TEAM DAD

Having worked with Drew Pittman in his role as an NFL agent, I can attest to his genuine character and integrity. When he told me he was writing a book on how to thrive as a husband and father, I knew this was a book I needed to read. Knowing Drew, I've been encouraged and challenged by his example and wisdom—read this book so you can get to know this man as well.

JOHN SCHNEIDER
Executive Vice President and General Manager, Seattle Seahawks

As a Christian NFL agent working in a secular industry, Drew Pittman brings a unique perspective on the family. In *First Team Dad*, his philosophy about football translates seamlessly to family values. To the football fan's delight, Drew shares behind-the-scenes stories about his experiences with famous players and coaches in order to demonstrate practical points about having a strong family. I believe every man who reads this book will walk away inspired and will have a game plan for his own family.

ROBERT MORRIS
Founding Senior Pastor, Gateway Church, Dallas, Texas
Bestselling Author of *The Blessed Life*, *From Dream to Destiny* and *The God I Never Knew*

Drew Pittman's book *First Team Dad* will be a benefit to fathers as they lead their families. As coaches, we believe in fundamentals—and that is exactly what Drew recommends to those who wish to become the fathers they should be and the leaders of their homes.

BOB STOOPS
Head Football Coach, Oklahoma Sooners
BCS National Champions and Orange Bowl Victors, 2000

The heart of each of the 30 chapters of *First Team Dad* is based on the sound, solid principles of coaching a team to achieve success. Coaching our family teams to success is not only our responsibility, but also our duty as leaders in our homes.

SCOTT DREW
Head Men's Basketball Coach, Baylor University Bears
Austin American Statesman's Coach of the Year Award, 2010

As a collegiate football coach and executive director of the American Football Coaches Association, I have long held a strong belief that coaches become surrogate fathers to many of their players. However, a coach's roles as father and husband in his home are his first responsibilities. Drew Pittman's book, *First Team Dad*, is not only a great resource for coaches and teachers, but also for fathers out there who are striving to become positive leaders in their home.

GRANT TEAFF
Executive Director, American Football Coaches Association
Former Head Football Coach, Baylor University Bears
College Football Hall of Fame, 2001

As coaches we often have a responsibility to become surrogate fathers and role models for some of our players. As important as that is, our essential role is to be a father to our own children and a husband to our wife. *First Team Dad* recommends 30 methods to help men better their marriages and to become a first team dad for their children.

DAVID CUTCLIFFE
Head Football Coach, Duke University Blue Devils

Coaches have to consciously make an effort to become what Drew Pittman describes in his new book, *First Team Dad*. There is no greater satisfaction than seeing your players become the kind of men they are capable of being; and there is no greater joy than teaching your own children to develop a positive set of values and seeing them live by that value system as adults.

MACK BROWN
Former Head Football Coach, University of Texas at Austin Longhorns
Paul "Bear" Bryant Award for Coach of the Year, 2006

First Team Dad is a must-read for any man who wants to improve as a father and husband. Drew's book is a fascinating, self-reflecting, easy read that will inspire and motivate men to take action. It's not the type of book you read once and put on the shelf; rather it's a daily reference and guide. Drew is a man of high character and a committed husband and father. It's a blessing and gift that he has so eloquently shared his personal experiences and valuable lessons and insight. I feel challenged and motivated to apply Drew's principles to my life.

ROB BRZEZINSKI
Vice President, Football Operations, Minnesota Vikings

The most revealing endorsement for a book sharing tools that will help marriages, parenting and the home is a glimpse into the life and home of the author—to see if he puts into practice what he's written and then, to see the results. The endorsement of my friend Drew Pittman's life and family convinces me that the tools and principles in this book work. *First Team Dad* provides a compelling look into the principles of football and applies those principles to our homes. Drew provides this insight without being preachy or judgmental. It is a great playbook for any family to improve their home.

JOE CHAMPION
Pastor, Celebration Church, Georgetown, Texas

I first met Drew in 2009 while I was going through the agent process. He was honest, patient, and most important, a man of God. Six years into our relationship, he continues to coach me in different avenues of my life: my marriage, my children, my career and being a man of faith trying to survive in a fast-paced world. The life lessons in *First Team Dad* are no different.

JARED COOK
Tight End, NFL

Drew Pittman's *First Team Dad* provides a winning playbook for Super Bowl-style parenting. With biblical truth, practical applications and powerful examples from Drew's many years working with NFL coaches and players, this book will inspire every reader to a new level of leading and loving his children.

CHRIS HODGES
Senior Pastor, Church of the Highlands, Grants Mill, Alabama
Author of *Fresh Air* and *Four Cups*

As a dad I need powerful, meaningful, and easy wins for my relationship with my kids. I can't settle for family field goals when I need touchdowns! Drew Pittman has thrown all us dads an "on the numbers," tear drop pass for six with *First Team Dad*. His intuitive sense of masculinity and his magnetic use of sport to grab the essence of fatherhood make his real-life solutions resonate.

KENNY LUCK
Men's Pastor, Saddleback Church
Founder, Every Man Ministries
Author, *Sleeping Giant*

Not everybody is naturally a great dad and husband. Some people need some guidance, not me of course, but some guys. Seriously though, I've known Drew for a while now and I know the integrity with which he manages his athletes. I love the inside look he gives us into the sports agent world, and how those stories relate to our homes is really cool and very helpful. You will enjoy reading *First Team Dad*.

BART MILLARD
Lead Singer, MercyMe

I have known Drew for nearly 15 years. He has a true passion not only for his own family but also for helping other men be stronger husbands and fathers. This book is a great game plan for men of any age who wish to propel their marriage and parenting role from good to great. *First Team Dad* was an encouragement to me and a reminder of the dedication necessary to maintain a healthy home. I recommend you read it too.

TAYLOR MORTON
Director of Player Personnel, St. Louis Rams

As a veteran NFL coach, it was always important to me to draft young men who had character and integrity. Through the ministry of the Fellowship of Christian Athletes, we are influencing young men and women to build their lives on Christian principles and seeking to reflect those same values in our own lives. To that end, Drew Pittman, as a successful NFL agent in a competitive and challenging business, has made a difference by impacting and shaping his clients into men of strong character. *First Team Dad* is written by a special man who refuses to teach *winning at all costs*. Much to learn here—wisdom we can all use regardless of our own field of play.

LES STECKEL
President and CEO, Fellowship of Christian Athletes

Strong families don't just happen; they are built, slowly and carefully. In *First Team Dad* you'll find the tools you need to begin to build an enduring legacy for your family. Read the book and watch as God begins to work in your life and in the lives of your family.

GREG SURRATT
Senior Pastor, Seacoast Church, Author, *Ir-rev-rend*

FOREWORD BY **TONY DUNGY**

FIRST TEAM DAD

YOUR PLAYBOOK FOR A WINNING FAMILY

J. DREW PITTMAN

BETHANY HOUSE
a division of Baker Publishing Group
www.BethanyHouse.com

Published by Bethany House Publishers
11400 Hampshire Avenue South
Bloomington, Minnesota 55438
www.bethanyhouse.com

Bethany House Publishers is a division of
Baker Publishing Group, Grand Rapids, Michigan
www.bakerpublishinggroup.com

Printed in the United States of America

Library of Congress Cataloging-in-Publication Data is on file at the
Library of Congress, Washington, DC.

Published in association with the literary agency of Wolgemuth & Associates, Inc.

14 15 16 17 18 19 20 | 7 6 5 4 3 2 1

To my Dad, John H. Pittman,
who went to be with the Lord on December 17, 2013.
I was blessed to have a Dad who loved me unconditionally and taught me
so many valuable lessons. I miss you every day. I am grateful for
the influence you had in my life. You are a part of a legacy
that will last until Jesus returns.

Contents

Foreword

By Tony Dungy

I've known Drew Pittman for almost 20 years. Our friendship has blossomed from a very unlikely source: football. You're probably thinking, *What's so unlikely about two men developing a friendship around football?*—especially since both of us have worked around the game for most of our adult lives. However, the jobs we have performed should have placed us at odds with each other.

For 28 years I was a coach in the National Football League; Drew was an agent who represented players. I represented management, a group often portrayed as only interested in getting the most from the players while keeping the costs of players' services down. This included effectively managing the salary cap so that their team had the best chance to win. Agents, on the other hand, are often seen as operating solely for their clients—determined to maximize their players' salaries without concern for anything else. Theoretically, that would put us on opposite sides of the field.

Stories of animosity, bad blood and mistrust between team representatives and agents are legendary in the league, and I'm sure, in some cases, well deserved. I never experienced that in my dealings with Drew. This was simply because, as Christians, neither one of us modeled those stereotypical roles. We felt we had a higher calling: It was our job to help our players grow as athletes and as people, and to do what we could to help *everyone* succeed. We understood that, while I had a responsibility to my team and he had a responsibility to his players, we were both ultimately working for the Lord. Knowing that, we didn't have to be adversaries—we could work together to achieve both of our goals. So, over the years, our friendship has grown because of our shared relationship in Christ and we never allowed business to weaken that bond.

We also realized that we had another common interest: seeing men lead their families properly and helping those families grow stronger. Working with so many young men allowed us see that, as a whole, we dads weren't doing a great job of preparing our children for life. Because helping men become better husbands and fathers has been a passion for me over the years, I was excited to hear that Drew was working on this book.

First Team Dad addresses many of the problems we are facing in America with our families. Rather than just enumerating the problems, this book gives practical, biblical solutions to men on how to correct them. This book uses illustrations from football and principles from coaching a team and applies them to leading a family. Because we are so passionate about the sport, many men will relate to these concepts and I believe that applying them will help us as we fight to turn things around in our homes, schools and communities.

Family life and family values have taken a hit in our society and it is going to take work to restore them. Just as turning a football team from a loser into a winner begins with a shift in thinking, so too rebuilding our families starts with changing our culture and our mindset. In *First Team Dad*, Drew lays out a game plan of biblical principles that are easy to understand, and applying them will help you create this change in your family. Every one of us wants to guide our family in the best way possible. We want our wives to love us and our kids to grow into thriving adults. Whether you're doing a great job of that or whether you're struggling at being a husband and a father, this book will help.

It's my hope that by reading *First Team Dad* you will be motivated to do a better job of leading your family and that you will reach out to other men you know to help them catch this vision. Together we can be on the same team, working on that higher calling to build better families and, ultimately, a better country.

Preface

I have read many great books by many very smart people. Maybe it's just me, but one of my frustrations is getting to the end of the book and not having a clue how to implement any of what I have just read. That is why at the end of every chapter of *First Team Dad*, there is a Game Plan. The Game Plan is a strategy for implementing the material. It is not a magic formula that guarantees your family will be transformed overnight, but it is a guide to help you get the ball rolling.

Every family is different, so your biggest areas of need will probably be different from those of your best friend or the guy down the street. I suggest reading through the whole book first, and then going back and starting to implement the Game Plans. You don't have to start at chapter 1 and then move on to chapter 2. If a chapter jumps out at you as the place to start, start there. I would also suggest that you do not simply read the book and put it on a shelf. Keep it out and refer back to it. I highly encourage you to have your wife read this book also. You will need to be on the same page, and you will need her support in order to successfully implement the principles discussed. If you are divorced and not living with your kids every day, give your ex-wife a copy and communicate as best you can about the strategies. If you are part of a small group, you could go through it together as a study.

You might read a chapter and think, *I can do that* or *I can make that happen* and then your family looks at you like you are crazy. Change is not always people's favorite thing. I encourage you to be intentional. I hope you are very excited about the different strategies and suggestions in this book, and that you see the value in each one. Just understand that at the beginning your family may not see the same vision you see. Casting vision for any group is an ongoing process. Be creative. Figure out how to work things in without having a big family meeting with a "we are making *big changes around here*" announcement.

To be candid with you, I am currently dealing with the challenge of having my boys show respect. They are a little too much like my wife and me in that they are confident, sure of themselves, and comfortable in their own skin. All of these traits are going to serve them well in life, but for now they are not mature enough to know when to turn that down a notch and just do what we tell them to do, when we tell them to do it. So we are struggling with their thinking that they get to run their own show and do things on their schedule. I have to follow my own advice by being consistent with what I expect and by being persistent.

The intent of this book is to initiate lifestyle change to bring about greatness in your home. I encourage you to take each suggestion individually and implement them one at a time. There are some suggestions that must start with you and some that are for the whole family. Chapter 1 ("Redefine Success") is one that you may need to get a handle on for yourself before showing your family how to define success. You can start on that and simultaneously move into chapter 17 ("Let Your Faith Be Infectious"), which could be something your whole family works on at once. You can be working on your definition of success while you and your family determine the best way to have infectious faith.

Just try to stay away from piling too much change on your family at once. That could get overwhelming for everybody. It is like working out. You can't go to the gym benching 100 pounds and expect to throw up 400 pounds in one week. You have to go in every day, get over the initial soreness, build up some stamina, and stay with it. You might go from benching 100 pounds to 110 then 120. . . and before you know it, you are at 200. You will make big gains in some months, and in others you may fight to maintain your current weight max—but you keep showing up. Or it can be like dieting. If you starve yourself for a week and get on the scales expecting a huge drop, you will most likely be disappointed. To effect big change, you must change your eating habits—how much you eat, what types of food you eat, when you eat—until eating right is simply what you do. Over time, you will drop weight and lose inches in the right places.

As in a workout program or a plan to change your eating habits, your implementation of *First Team Dad* will ebb and flow. There will be great victories that produce great results. There will also be times of frustration. If you fly through the first 10 chapters and see great success, but then have an issue with "Controlling the Pace" as a result of an unforeseen work deadline or some overlap in the kid's schedules, don't sweat it. Move on to another chapter and come back to "Controlling the Pace" when things ease up.

Now the fun part begins! You get to start the process and see how your family changes. The dynamics will shift before your eyes. Some behaviors will change quickly, while others. . . well, not so much. Do not get discouraged. Sometimes I laugh to myself, as my family does not respond as I wish they would and as I expect them to respond. I ponder what people would think if they saw that the author doesn't always get the great results. Just know that overall it is working. Be consistent and persevere through the frustration and the slow reactions.

I hope you enjoy the stories from my experiences as an NFL agent. I have had a great time over the last 22 years in this industry. At least, most of it has been great. I believe God has worked through Craig Domann, my business partner, and me. I believe there are many reasons God has allowed me to be an agent and live out these unique experiences. I believe He knows I want to be the faithful leader these players need in their lives. I believe the fact that you are reading this book shows that you want to be the faithful leader your family needs. I believe God wants you to achieve greatness in your home and He wants your family to be a winning family. God bless you and God bless your family!

—Drew Pittman

Introduction

That Pivotal Moment

In every game, there is a pivotal moment when the momentum shifts and split-second decisions determine whether the game will be won or lost. That instant in time may only consume a few seconds on the game clock, but its impact alters the entire outcome. Life is surprisingly similar to sports. My pivotal moment came on December 31, 1992.

I was living in a suburb of Dallas, Texas, at the time, and I was stuck at home suffering from the flu. Lying flat in my bed and encased in blankets, I flipped on the TV in a flu-induced haze and landed on one of the day's bowl games. Baylor University and the University of Arizona were about to face off in the John Hancock Bowl. Rain was pouring from the sky, drenching the more than 41,000 fans gathered in El Paso's Sun Bowl Stadium.

As the teams warmed up, the announcers broke down the upcoming game. Much was being made of the fact that this would be the last game of Baylor head coach Grant Teaff's storied career. The broad-shouldered bull of a man was leaving the game a legend.

When Coach Teaff had arrived on campus in 1972, the Baylor Bears were a dreadful team from a private Christian college located in Central Texas. Coach Teaff had been a little-known football coach at Angelo State University when Baylor called. He was their fifth or sixth choice, and many boosters expected him to fail, just as his predecessors had. But Coach Teaff didn't let the naysayers discourage him. He took the cast-off recruits that bigger schools didn't want, and he won with them.

During his 21-year tenure at the school, Coach Teaff transformed Baylor into a respectable program that was competing with major state schools in the illustrious Southwest Conference.

He became known as a master motivator, and Baylor fans still tell the story of his eating a worm in the locker room to fire up his team. His unlikely snack illustrated that he was willing to do whatever it took to win, and players never questioned his commitment after that display.

As the winter raindrops fell on that December day, Coach Teaff again found himself facing off against the naysayers. Arizona was heavily favored to win the bowl game, but Coach Teaff—in characteristic fashion—seemed not to notice. He opened the game with a risky flea flicker and shortly thereafter ran a fake punt against Arizona's "Desert Storm," the second-ranked defense in the nation. A fantastic game took shape, and for nearly four hours, my feverish eyes were glued to the television screen. When the final game gun sounded, the Bears had won, 20 to 15. The team had prevailed in Coach Teaff's finale.

During his 21 seasons at Baylor, Coach Teaff compiled 128 wins—more than any coach in the history of the program. He won 2 conference championships, appeared in 8 bowl games, and would be inducted into the College Football Hall of Fame 9 years later.

The cameras were fixed on this retiring icon as the game ended and his team gave him the traditional Gatorade bath at midfield and swept him off his feet. They began to carry him off the field—and then something extraordinary happened that was forever burned into my memory. Coach Teaff signaled for the team to put him down. He then walked over to the sidelines and motioned for his wife and three daughters to meet him on the field. Grabbing their hands, he left the game the same way he had entered it: as a man who loved his family and never lost sight of what was important.

As I watched the conclusion to this man's coaching career, I began to weep. *Wow. This is what family is supposed to look like*, I thought, while tears streamed down my cheeks. *Here is a man who could have been exalted by his team and carried off the field, but he chose to exit the game with those people who meant the most to him instead.*

One reason that memory still moves me is that I've always loved the pageantry of athletics. You could say that my love for sports is in my blood. I grew up watching and playing nearly every sport imaginable. I have been a faithful follower of the Dallas Cowboys since the age of six; as season ticket holders, my dad and

I made it to every game we could. In college, I played soccer for Southern Methodist University. Decades earlier, my dad had played basketball for Texas Tech, and my grandfather, Melvin O. Pittman, strapped on a leather helmet with the Pittsburgh Steelers in 1935 at the age of 27. I'm part of a rich sports heritage and love sports so much I've tied my livelihood to it.

But the memory of that 1992 bowl game has stuck with me for a greater reason than just its significance in sports history. While my own father had taught me many lessons on the importance of being a strong leader, it was in the moment at the Sun Bowl that I first saw a public figure openly display the powerful impact that a strong father can have on creating a healthy family. This thought has left such a profound impression on me that I often say that the John Hancock Bowl may have been played on the last day of that year, but in many ways, it marks the first day of my life as the leader of a household. Coach Teaff knew that one's effort in the office or on the field is not nearly as important as one's contribution to the home.

Interestingly, my passions for sports and family have merged in my work as an NFL sports agent. I knew it would be next to impossible for me to break into the sports representation industry when I started my company from scratch; this business is cut-throat in every sense of the word. So I decided to conduct myself differently. I wanted to be honest and ethical—to never break a rule. My business has two major components: recruiting new clients and managing existing careers. There are moments in every recruiting process when you feel pressure to lie or manipulate to get the client. You tell yourself that *this* will be the player who puts you over the top . . . so maybe it's worth bending the rules just this once. I've never given in to that temptation, however, and I'm proud to have kept my moral commitment for more than 22 years. My firm has negotiated nearly a billion dollars in contracts for players, proving that walking the high road is not always an occupational suicide mission.

My career has also kept my passion for healthy families burning. I've been able to peek behind the curtain of professional sports in ways few others get to do. What I've found is that the world of professional sports is a microcosm of the rest of society. The teams who win consistently and the teams who finish at the bottom of the standings every year do so for similar reasons: the quality of their leadership. On the player side, I'm astounded by the number of men who come from broken homes and by those who seem bent on perpetuating the cycle of brokenness. Many lack a true sense of what it means to be a man. They have sex with multiple partners, have children with more than one of them, and end up saturating their kids' lives with absence. Even those who are physically present are often emotionally absent. While their children tug at their pant legs, they are talking on their phones, checking email, or just clearly uninterested. Many of these men approach family with a sense of entitlement rather than responsibility. The children who crave their fathers' attention can't get it. They are twisting the doorknobs of their fathers' hearts but can't get inside. Sadly, the NFL is flush with absent fathers, unloving husbands and poor leaders. It's not hard to understand why. The business is so time-consuming that it is hard for these men—players, coaches, office personnel, staff members—to spend quality time with their families.

Unfortunately, broken families are not just filling the National Football League; they are flooding neighborhoods across America. Marriage itself is now in decline, and more people are choosing to cohabitate or avoid relational commitments altogether. This means more children are born out of wedlock and are growing up in unstable situations. Couples who do choose to marry are divorcing at unacceptably high rates, which has created a fatherlessness epidemic in America that is causing untold damage to children. Children from fatherless homes are 15.3 times more likely to have behavioral disorders, 4.6 times more likely to commit suicide, 24.3 times more likely to run away, 6.3 times more likely to end up in state-operated institutions, and 6.6 times more likely to drop out of school than those who are raised by both of their parents.[1] Regardless of the cause, the American family is hurting and we need a new game plan.

I was raised in a wonderful home with a supportive mother and a father who was involved in my life. At the same time, I experienced the pain from my parents' divorce at a young age. I personally know the benefits of a healthy home as well as the difficulties caused by a broken family.

—++++++++—

About a year after that Sun Bowl game, I sent in a $150 check to the State of Texas to incorporate as a sports agent. Around that time, a good friend of mine told me that he wanted to introduce me to a girl he worked with. He thought she might be able to help as I started this new venture, because her father was a well-respected "football man." Her name? Layne Teaff. Just three months after our introduction, I was engaged to one of the women I'd seen walk off the field with her father, Coach Grant Teaff, that flu-stricken day. Today, Layne and I have two sons and a dog named Gracie. I've had a lot of successes as a father and more failures than I care to admit, but my heart has never stopped burning with the desire to create a healthy home for my kids and to set an example for them by loving and honoring my wife. Applying helpful principles I've learned from sports to my family has helped me achieve both of these goals.

Today, I have a picture in my office of Coach Teaff and his wife, Donell, walking off the field together. It is a reminder to me of his legacy—not just as a coach, but also as a husband, father and community leader. He always says his life has been lived for faith, family and football—and *always* in that order. He would also tell you that the principles that made him successful in football also made him successful at home.

In my life and work, I've found Coach Teaff's point proved true again and again. Competitive sports are filled with lessons about motivation, perseverance, hard work and collaboration—and these lessons are powerfully transferable to everyday life. Yet not nearly enough men apply these principles to the most important arena they'll ever play in: the home. You don't need to be an athlete to learn and use these lessons; in the pages that follow, I will share with you a series of "game changers" that can improve your family life. I've picked up these principles from spending my life as an insider in the world of sports, and I've tested them with great success in my own home.

Because you're still reading, I suspect you're a lot like me. You want to be a better dad and a more loving husband. You want to construct a happy home and build a winning family. You want to be a better leader and learn how to balance the many demands of the modern world. More than anything, when your final gun sounds and you walk off the field called "life," you want to know you've left a legacy worth remembering.

Note

1. Statistics compiled by Fathers Unite. http://fathersunite.org/statistics_on_father lessnes.html (accessed March 2014).

1

Redefine Success

Mike Minter was an all-conference safety for the University of Nebraska Cornhuskers. His sheer athleticism made him an invaluable playmaker, and he played a key role in helping his team to win the first back-to-back consensus national championships in 40 years. After my partner, Craig Domann, negotiated his second deal with the Carolina Panthers, Mike told us a story I'll never forget.

By the time he started his junior season at Nebraska, Mike had set his sights on the National Football League. But during a big game, he planted his leg and heard the sound no player ever wants to hear: a pop that sounded like a gun going off in the cold, dark night. Mike fell to the turf. When he regained his senses, he realized that his career might be slipping through his fingers. He was lying on a carpet of grass, staring up at the stars, as team trainers and managers examined his injury. Time began to slow. Sounds swirled. His mind churned.

Am I done with all of this? he asked himself. *If so, is there more out there for me, or is football all there is?*

A young man who had spent his entire life thinking that football would be his life now began to reconsider everything. As he was helped off the field, the fragility of his situation hit him between the eyes. In that moment, he made up his mind to stop chasing after what the world calls "success" and to begin pursuing a life of true significance.

Against all odds, Mike Minter returned to the game of football and had a long, successful career in the NFL. But he never played the same. He always reminded himself that football was not an end but a means to something greater. He had come to believe that God blesses us not so we can hold onto it but so that we can give to others. While many of his teammates were out trying to work endorsement deals or sign autographs, Mike was engaged in community service and volunteer work. He recently left Liberty University, a large Christian college, and took the position of head football coach at Campbell University, where he "trains young champions for Christ."

As parents, the way you and I live our lives teaches our children what is important in life. If you work long hours and sacrifice family time, they will notice. If you choose more money over the opportunity to coach their Little League team, that will communicate something to them. It's easy to plan your family around your schedule, but it's harder to plan your schedule around your family. Yet the choices you make ripple through their lives and shape the legacy you'll leave behind. They will remember the late-night conversations over a cereal bowl more than any toy you buy them.

Are you teaching your kids to chase after success or to pursue significance? Sometimes a success-driven mindset appears to be good parenting. We live in a results-oriented society. But instead of measuring the results only, parents must observe the process. We must measure the behavior that leads to results. We often pressure our children to make good grades, thrive in sports, and pursue extracurricular activities. But are we investing in their lives? Are we pushing them to pursue what they love, even if it has no immediate or tangible result? I have a friend with a 15-year-old daughter in high school. She tells him that the pressure to take AP classes and excel at extracurricular activities is burdensome. Her school counselors advise students to beef up their resumes so they'll make it into a good college.

The same is often true for our marriages. We can become hyper-focused on results—frequency of sex, amount of monthly income, number of arguments in a given month. These become the only measures of our marriage's health. We forget to focus on living a better story and loving more deeply. My wife and I have some friends who have been married for more than 20 years. We went to dinner with these friends awhile back and asked them how they were doing. He had recently started a new position at the same company, and she was juggling teenagers—a 14-year-old boy and an 18-year-old girl. Their daughter is about to head off to college, which brings about a whole new set of stresses. Their response was interesting.

They are both great people and not people you would look at and have immediate concerns about their relationship. His response was about his new position at work; hers was about the kids. We rephrased the question with the emphasis on how *they* were doing. This time, the response was about his lack of time to work out and her desire to get more involved in some areas of their church. We finally were blunt and to the point: "How is your relationship with each other?"

They didn't really know how to answer. They smiled at each other but didn't know what to say. Finally, he responded that they didn't have any issues and were getting along just fine. They had scheduled Wednesday night as their night to have sex, expressing that if they didn't put it on the schedule it wouldn't get done. She said they really weren't arguing at all, joking that they didn't see each other enough to have anything to fight about. They agreed that money was going to be a little tight with their daughter going off to school but they had discussed how to handle that issue. They smiled, patted each other on the shoulder, and confirmed that all was good.

I couldn't help but feel like I had just witnessed an impromptu business meeting in which department heads had concluded that their departments were productive and cooperative and had figured out a way to work together to improve their revenue and expense issues. I know our friends are not the only case like this. I feel many marriages are results driven and are merely hollow shells of what a healthy marriage should be.

The average length of employment in the NFL is 2.3 years. So when I sign a player, I don't just want to help him become "successful." I want to position him for significance. Success is a destination that's often surprisingly easy to reach, while significance is a lifestyle that is far more difficult to maintain. As with my players, if you learn to focus on living a life of significance—and if you help your children do the same—the impact of your life will stretch far beyond your years.

One of our firm's proudest moments in more than two decades of sports representation was the day Mike Minter announced his retirement. The press conference was packed, and as Mike broke the news, the owner of the Carolina Panthers cried. He knew he was losing one of the greatest men on his team. Unlike many of his teammates, Mike had learned that true success could not be calculated in wins and losses.

GamePlan

- Ask your children to rank what is most important in life: relationships, God, money or fame. Talk with them about why they chose each one.

- For a typical week, calculate the time you spend with your spouse, children, friends, and at work. Do you need to make any changes?

- Plan with your family to do a good deed that has no tangible benefit except to the person you bless. As a family, share what was meaningful about the experience.

2

Create a Culture

At the 2010 American Football Coaches Association's convention in Orlando, Florida, I listened with rapt attention to one of the most profound speeches I'd ever heard. Coach Nick Saban had just won the BCS National Championship at the University of Alabama and was asked to deliver the keynote address to a room of 10,000 football coaches. The room waited in silence as Saban opened with eight simple words: "The way we do it at our place . . ." And then he outlined the non-negotiables for those who are a part of his team. By knowing what you're building towards, Saban pointed out, you can achieve great progress. What is true for the Crimson Tide family is true for your family. All great coaches are successful at building an intentional culture, and great parents must do likewise. They must create a culture that embodies and prioritizes what matters most to them.

When Coach Saban took over at Alabama in 2007, the Crimson Tide had been embroiled in a string of issues that had chipped away at the core of one of the most storied football programs in the country. The Tide lost head coach Dennis Franchione to Texas A&M while under NCAA scrutiny. Next was a one-year stint under Mike Price that resulted in his dismissal revolving around some indiscretions off the field. When Mike Shula took over the program, the NCAA sanctions had come down, and devastating injuries to key players kept Alabama well below the winning record alumni had come to expect. Then, in 2007, Saban was tapped from the Miami Dolphins to return the program to national prominence.

Not an easy task and not one a veteran leader like Nick Saban took lightly. When discussing the first steps he took upon his arrival in Tuscaloosa, Coach Saban explained that everyone from the guys who painted the stripes on the famous Bryant-Denny Stadium field to the president of the University had to buy in or the turnaround would fall short. But if everyone would embrace "the way," he promised to bring the Crimson Tide an opportunity to play for National Championships.

How do you "do it at your place"? What is your culture? Do you know what it is? Does your family know what it is? The foundation of your leadership must start with what you stand for and who *your* leader is. In my house the foundation is Jesus Christ. We stand for truth, character and integrity. We are teammates, we serve one another, and we are disciplined. I would love to say that we are always really good at all of these things. We are not. We all fail from time to time. But we have a vision of what we want our family dynamic to look like, and we know that our failings do not invalidate the culture of our home. We can recognize our shortcomings and improve. With a house full of young boys, it sometimes seems like a losing battle, but we have a strong foundation and we are all on the same page. Our culture was not something mandated by me or my wife. No, we sat down as a family and discussed how we wanted our life together to be.

Now, in our homes, we can't send our kids packing if they don't buy into the culture like Coach Saban can! I know, sometimes we'd like to. So it's a little trickier. Also, it's harder to get buy-in when your team members are 4 or 10 or even 15 years old. The best thing we can do is to establish the culture early and model it ourselves. If you haven't done so yet and your kids are older, start now and get them involved. If your family has input into the process, they will take ownership. But if you impose a set of guidelines or a bunch of dos and don'ts, you won't get the desired results. Though the results of living by the culture might *appear* similar to abiding by a list of rules, the difference is evident in the way the system is conceived and implemented.

Coach Saban had to overcome the underachievement and NCAA infractions that had plagued the Alabama football program. The program had suffered a string of losing seasons, attendance was down, enrollment was down, and the pride that had once been associated with Alabama football was nowhere to be found. Coach Saban knew he had to start at the foundational level to regain the success to which the program was accustomed. So he created his culture and called it "The Process." Saban was quoted as saying,

> Do you want to be the best you can be? Are you driven to be the best player you can be? Are you driven to have the intensity, the sense of urgency, the intelligence? Are you going to work to do the things you need to do to be your absolute best?[1]

He knew those were the characteristics necessary for his players and the Alabama program to be their best. His Process is as follows:

- *Discipline*: doing what you're supposed to do, when you're supposed to do it, how it's supposed to be done.
- *Effort:* straining your gut on every play.
- *Commitment:* you will either suffer the pain of discipline or the pain of disappointment.
- *Toughness:* never show weakness.
- *Pride:* how good do you want to be?[2]

Every time I read "The Process," I want to suit up for Coach Saban. How could I not be motivated to achieve greatness when I'm set up to be my absolute best? It is no wonder he has had such success. It would be hard to go to Alabama on a recruiting visit and leave without committing. But Coach Saban didn't have the string of National Championships when he got there. He didn't have the winning streaks or even a record he could talk about. He had to start from scratch. Maybe you can relate because you are in that place.

 In your home, what is the way you do it at your place? Does everyone know what is expected of them? Does everyone buy in? Do you model this behavior? Do you and your family know what the outcome of being your best will be—the benefits of striving for and achieving greatness? If you don't know what your culture is, or you don't have buy-in, start over. This is the beginning of greatness. This is the foundation. Without the foundation, the other pieces are irrelevant.

GamePlan

- Identify what you think your family should stand for and what is worth striving for. What are your non-negotiable values?

- As a family, identify the foundational cornerstones of your family's culture. Post your ideas in the house, everywhere.

- Talk about the benefits of living out your culture and decide what should happen when someone on the team doesn't live by the agreed-upon principles.

Notes

1. "Quotable Quotes by Nick Saban," Tide Football. http://www.tidefootball.com/pages.php?page=07/01/23/4711690 (accessed April 2014). See also www.coachsaben.net, "The Process."
2. Nick Saban with Brian Curtis, *How Good Do You Want to Be?* (New York: Ballantine, 2007), pp. 31-32, adapted. See also www.coachsaben.net, "The Process."

3

Construct a Game Plan

Small, private Christian schools are usually not known as sports powerhouses. These schools don't often compete in major conferences, and they are finding it more and more difficult to even remain in the big conferences. Baylor University has long been the underdog in a big conference. First they were in the old Southwest Conference (SWC), competing against the likes of the University of Texas, Texas A&M, the University of Arkansas and Texas Tech University. When the Big 12 was formed by combining the Big 8 and the SWC, Baylor surprisingly found itself once again competing against most of the above-mentioned SWC schools along with the University of Oklahoma, Oklahoma State, the University of Kansas and Kansas State. It had been thought that Baylor would be cast off with the other small private schools when the Big 12 was created. Not so.

My father-in-law, Grant Teaff, was the head football coach at Baylor University for 21 seasons. Over the course of his career, Teaff coached many teams with inferior talent to victory. How? By constructing a superior game plan. He had a staff of smart and cunning coaches who would find ways to beat the bigger schools with their better facilities and, more important, higher-caliber athletes. One such game was the 1974 contest against the University of Texas. Based just 90 miles south of Waco, the University of Texas Longhorns were a million miles away in terms of talent and accomplishment. The Longhorns owned the previous six conference championships and seemed to be well on their way to number seven when they got off the bus in Waco to face a Baylor team that was, well, *not* projected to win the conference. The Longhorns rolled into town with a three-game winning streak and a #12 national ranking. They got off to a 24-7 halftime lead and the Baylor faithful lost their faith. They filed out of Floyd Casey stadium, not willing to witness another crushing defeat at the hands of the Longhorns.

But at halftime, Coach Teaff told his Bears they had the Longhorns right where they wanted them. A little past the halfway point of the season, with UT facing a tough road game at TCU the following week, followed by the always brutal game versus "step-brother" Texas A&M, Coach Teaff told his staff to expect the Darrell Royal-led Longhorns to come out with many of their second teamers. Teaff predicted that overconfidence and the expected substitutions by the Longhorns would give the Bears the opportunity to jump out strong and create momentum that could not be stopped before it was too late.

Sure enough, a blocked punt started the momentum shift, and the seemingly overconfident Longhorns couldn't stop the momentum. The carefully executed game plan Coach Teaff and his staff had devised was working as planned. The fans climbing into their cars in the parking lot heard the roars bursting out of the stands and quickly returned to their seats. People who were already in their cars heading home turned around and poured back into the stadium. The Bears went on to post an amazing 34-24 victory and kick-started a dream season that was later dubbed "The Miracle on the Brazos." The Bears won the conference that year. Coach Teaff started a legacy that eventually led to Baylor being included in the Big 12 and landed him in the College Football Hall of Fame. The power of a great game plan cannot be underestimated.

It's the same with your family. If your culture is what you value, then your game plan is how you establish that culture throughout the life of your family. If you want to be successful in creating a healthy family environment, you'd better have an intentional game plan. I call it the FGP, short for Family Game Plan. Your wife is both your offensive and defensive coordinator. She should be heavily involved in the creation of the game plan if you expect her to help you execute it. But you need to stay involved as well. Too often men delegate all of this to their wives. And while it's easy to point out the things that you don't like in the family operations, you can't just stay out of the way most of the time and jump in only when something isn't going the way you want it to go. Being hands-off about the FGP doesn't work any better than creating the FGP by yourself and then lording it over your wife and kids. Getting input from the players, your kids, can be beneficial. Let them feel a sense of ownership, in age-appropriate ways, by giving them opportunities to have input.

The FGP might address any number of areas of family life:

- Treatment of one another
- Respect
- Serving
- Selflessness and selfishness
- A behavioral code of conduct
- Extending and receiving forgiveness
- School requirements (homework, grades, effort)
- Manners
- Responsibilities
- Consequences
- Rewards
- Extracurricular activities
- Taking care of one's belongings
- Church
- Freedoms
- Exercise
- Health and nutrition
- Hygiene
- Leadership

There are many more possibilities, and no two FGP's will be the same. Your FGP should be fluid; it should change as your family's situation changes—especially as your kids get older and as more freedoms are earned. You can be as detailed as you need, and you can solicit input from the kids as you see fit. In football, it is often said that the team that wins the game is the one that makes the proper halftime adjustments. We have many halftimes in our lives. We have to make adjustments, and we are frequently required to call audibles at the line. The parents who can make the right adjustments are the ones who will succeed.

I suggest that every FGP include a Code of Conduct. Our kids need to know what we expect from them, and not just the general principles of being honest or treating people right. We must be specific and teach them how to apply those basic truths. In our family culture, we have included having a servant's heart, being disciplined and responsible, and living with character—so our Code of Conduct includes behaviors that support such a culture.

The Code of Conduct should include specifics about appropriate language; treatment of others; use of manners; and overall respect for authority, rules and laws. The Code of Conduct should also include definitions of character traits such as integrity and accountability. Of course, *you* need to live by the code too. Don't say disparaging things about Mom's cooking or make backhanded remarks about one child's behavior to another child. Treat your wife and kids with respect. Treat your own parents with respect. Say "please" and "thank you" and "yes, sir" and "no, sir" to your elders. You can't tell your kids to obey the law and then speed down the highway!

Our kids need to understand that each of us is a representative of the family name. Specifically, kids should be taught that how we behave individually reflects on the entire team. One of the great things college fraternities teach and instill in their "team" members is a pride of the name. I was an Alpha Tau Omega. I went through a lot to become a member of my fraternity and therefore it meant something to me. We need to instill in our kids that pride of ownership in our family name. This might mean that some of us need to take a little more pride of ownership ourselves.

You may not have a long lineage of men in your family who give you *reasons* for taking pride in your family's name. I understand that. If this is the case for you, now is the time to start the lineage. If you do not respect your family name, how can you expect your kids to respect it? Start with yourself. You could research your family name and find out what important members of society had your name. Determine if there is a family crest and either adopt it as your own or create a new one. Robert Lewis, in his outstanding book *Raising a Modern-Day Knight,* uses this technique in the process of training young men to become knights. He encourages fathers to use the family crest, either framing it to mount on the wall or even having family rings made utilizing the crest. Be mindful to guard against creating an unhealthy pride, but do encourage an appropriate appreciation for your family name.

Another important item for every FGP to include is instructions on consequences. One of my clients, Daniel Sepulveda, formerly the punter for the Pittsburgh Steelers, shared with me an early lesson that his father, Carlos, taught all the Sepulveda boys. He called it the Law of Consequences. Daniel said that his father always reminded him that there were consequences for every decision. Coming home late meant not getting to go out the next time. Daniel knew that engaging in the same behavior as some of his peers would carry stiffer consequences for him, and he had no desire to experience those consequences. As an adult, Daniel is one of the most outstanding men of character I have ever known. He learned his father's lessons well and has benefited from applying it. He has saved himself a great deal of heartache by learning how to make good decisions, in part because he was trained to consider the consequences of his actions.

I believe that leadership is a critical component to the well-being of individuals and our society. Therefore, leadership principles, in their varied facets, should be incorporated into every FGP. We teach our kids to respect leadership, to identify good and bad leadership, and to realize that they can be leaders and be *under* leadership at the same time. Leadership is not only for our sons. We should also teach our daughters to be leaders and to be able to identify a good leader. As Ecclesiastes says, there is a time for all things under the sun. Of course the most important leadership lesson we can give our children is to model *good* leadership ourselves; this includes accepting criticism and being accountable when we mess up.

A coach would never go to the stadium on game day, walk onto the field, huddle his team up before the kickoff, and say, "What do you guys want to run today?" Without a well-thought-out game plan, no team would stand a chance. The same is true for your team. If you wait until you ship your kids off to college or send them out into the workforce to say, "What type of person do you want to be?" you probably won't get the results you were hoping for. I admit, I waited way too long to come up with our FGP, and that has made it more difficult to implement. But I'm glad we started, and you will be too.

GamePlan

- Get started by getting your family game plan in writing. Review your cultural values and list actions you can take in the right direction. Get input from your wife and, most important, pray!

- With your family, take your ideas from the step above and create some specific rules, needs and wants that will help make them happen.

- Review the plan regularly as a family and address areas where you aren't hitting the mark. Don't point fingers. Identify where you have done well and where you have struggled. Adjust the plan as needed.

4

Affirm Your Teammates

Warren Belin has built a reputation as one of the best linebacker coaches in football. When he was a player at Wake Forest University, he developed a reputation for going hard all the time. While some of his teammates would take periods off in practice, or even take plays off during games (i.e., not play hard every play), Belin would give it 100 percent all the time.

As a coach at the University of Georgia, Coach Belin was blessed to coach some of the finest athletes in college football. Most of these young men had been recruited by all the top schools. They'd had head coaches coming to their high schools to sell them on the benefits of matriculating at their respective universities. More often than not, this process started when the players were just 15 or 16 years old. So they were used to being treated like "the man" and being catered to in every way. Going from salesman (trying to land recruits) to mentor is not an easy transition. College coaches are equal parts teacher, coach, mentor, disciplinarian, father figure, boss and friend.

Coach Belin is a man who knows when he needs to say, "That isn't good enough." He also knows his pupils are young men, so he corrects them in a way that gets his point across while building them up. Unfortunately, many coaches, at every level, haven't figured out this delicate balance. Coach Belin is known for being tough—*real tough*. But his correction comes in the form of a challenge to do better and is always followed with motivation. He can often be heard barking about needed improvements and thanking players for their hard work in the same breath. This is why players who are fortunate enough to play for him consider it an honor and look back on the experience as life changing, not only because of the benefits to their careers, but also—and even more so—because of the benenfits to them as men.

Coach Belin boasts many NFL players as disciples of the Belin school of linebacking. He went from Georgia to the Carolina Panthers and recently back to his alma mater, Wake Forest. Many of his former players still consult with him about their play and how to handle circumstances in their lives. And, when they feel like doing something the easy way, or feel like taking a play off, they hear that voice in their head—stern but encouraging—saying, *You're better than that. Don't quit now; you've come too far. We'll never be champions if we don't practice like champions.* All in that familiar tone of their coach, mentor and friend.

Isn't this what you want your relationship with your family to look like? When your kids move on in their lives and careers, don't you want them to hear the voice of Dad when faced with difficult circumstances and tough decisions? And shouldn't that voice guide them to make good decisions and take the high road? When they feel like "taking a play off," don't you want them to hear that challenge followed by motivation in a familiar voice—*your* voice? When your wife is juggling kids and work and things going on around the house, don't you want her to hear your voice affirming her and motivating her to push through? That's what great coaches do. They know how to mix affirmation in with their communication to motivate their players. They do it in a way that makes their players know, deep in their hearts, that they can do it. They let them know that good isn't good enough—because *great* is what they have inside of them.

As I began to feel the desire to improve my leadership in my home, I asked God to show me how to accomplish this. I felt the Holy Spirit nudging me to be more affirming in my communication. I was encouraged to start with my wife. At first I thought that was a little strange, as my wife is a strong and confident woman. She is not one to worry about what others think of her—which is something I find attractive. One evening I came downstairs from my office and found the boys sitting at the bar eating dinner. Layne was multi-tasking as usual, cleaning up the kitchen and preparing our plates to eat while finishing up a promotional DVD she had done for Women of Faith. I looked over her shoulder and immediately saw how incredible this DVD was.

I felt the Lord encourage me to take the opportunity to shower her with praise in front of the boys. I told them how awesome their mother was, what a great mom she was, and how talented she was. I asked them if they realized that the video she had done was for the largest women's ministry in the world and that millions of women would be impacted by her work. I told them that there would probably be many women who would come to know the Lord because of that one DVD their mother had made. I said she could probably go to Hollywood and work on feature films, making tons of money, but that she had chosen to do God's work and spend time with us instead. The more I lavished her with compliments, the more she beamed. I could see her whole body and spirit lift with everything I said.

But equally important was how my sons reacted. At first they thought I was being a little goofy (something they are used to), but more and more it began to sink in that their mother was special. They both love their mother and have great relationships with her, but there was something different in how they were looking at her now. The rest of the night, they treated her a little differently—with a little more respect. I wish I could say I have made this a regular practice, but the fact is, I haven't. This doesn't mean I don't see the benefit; but like many men, I just don't think about it as often as I should. I can promise you I am going to work at getting better about it.

Is there anyone who doesn't like to be affirmed? I have seen many great NFL players you would think would have all the confidence in the world (and they do) who still want and need to hear their coach say, "Great job!" or give them a hug after a great play. Do you watch the NFL? Why do you think the coaches are doing that all the time? It's not because they can't wait to get all sweaty hugging 300-pound players who could conceivably crush their ribs in the process. It's because coaches know who needs their affirmation. Your wife may need it, or she may just appreciate it— either way, it is good for her, and it is good for your kids to see you actively affirming her.

Just as Coach Belin's players needed to be affirmed, our kids need it too. If you are like me, you might feel like you are always getting after your kids. Turn out the lights. Pick up your clothes. Brush your teeth. Do your homework. Quit hitting your brother. Eat your dinner. Stop eating so much sugar. The list goes on and on. And, as you probably know, it is exhausting for everybody.

I'm working on this, trying to mix in affirmation with the correction. Instead of saying for the twentieth time in three days, "Pick up your room," I make an effort to talk to my kids away from the "scene of the crime." Maybe when we're driving somewhere and it's just me and the boys, I'll ask them why they think I want them to keep their rooms clean. I'll tell them about the importance of developing discipline and the role that discipline has had in my own life. I'll tell them how the atmosphere of our home is affected by the environment—and the environment is affected by how things are kept. In this communication, I always try to stress how smart they are and that they are capable of great things. I affirm their ability to develop good habits. I've found that I have difficulty in affirming them for something I think they should do without reminders, and I'm working to change this. Because I've also found that when their room is clean, and I tell them how great it looks and that I appreciate their work, this affirmation goes a long way toward helping them develop better habits.

I have to reiterate, though, that at least as important as affirming your kids, is being intentional about affirming your wife. I will never forget some neighbors we once had. The wife was constantly talking about how she felt like the cook, the maid, the taxi driver, the emergency fix-it person, etc. But the worst part of all was that she felt like none of her family members appreciated her. Her husband wasn't some chauvinist jerk who didn't care about her. He just wasn't in tune to her feelings, and he certainly did not affirm her as he should have.

Your wife and your kids need to know without a doubt how important your wife is to you. Proverbs 18:22 says that the man who finds a wife finds a good thing and obtains favor from the Lord. Your kids are not the next most important thing after your relationship with Christ. Your wife is. When you put your kids in front of your wife, it not only puts your wife in a bad position, but it also puts your kids in a bad position. They are not equipped to handle being more important to Daddy than Mommy is. They are not equipped to being more important to Mommy than Daddy is, either. You and your wife have to be in agreement that you will put each other first.

In contrast to my former neighbor who was out of touch with his wife, I recently heard a powerful account of a man affirming his wife. This man took some amazing steps to show his wife how valuable she was to him personally and to the family. He got his family together—his wife and three kids—and took them outside, under the shade of the big oak tree in their backyard, which was his wife's favorite place. He had her stand up while the rest of the family took a knee in front of her. He spent the next five minutes telling her how amazing she was and all the ways she was valued by him and by the family as a whole. He then had his children do the same thing. This act of honoring his wife made a profound impact on her, on their children, and even on his friend who told me the story.

Let's face it: If your relationship with your wife is not on track and is not flourishing, then you will be hard-pressed to lead your home to greatness. Life moves fast and we sometimes get lost in the pace. Most men are not the greatest at noticing and tending to the details. We might be pretty good at recalling the details of our jobs, or the details of a round of golf last week or even last month, or the details of a big bass we landed or a buck we shot, but we are not always great at the details of our relationships with our wives and kids. We are not always real intuitive either.

Not too long ago, I played golf with a client during the off-season. Afterward, we went to his house, sat out back, and talked about the round. We had both played pretty well, so we were excited to relax and relive the round, shot by shot, hole by hole. We went into great detail about each hole—the conditions, where our shots landed, and even what we were thinking and trying to do. After about an hour of this, his wife came out and asked if we had stopped to get the milk she had asked us to pick up. As we looked at each other, it was clear we had forgotten. She said, "I've been listening to you both relive in great detail every shot in 18 holes of golf, and you can't remember to stop and get milk?"

Ouch.

When it comes to our teammates, we need to play "show and tell." We need to *show* them how special they are and we need to *tell* them the same. We can do this in small ways, like remembering to pick up milk. We can do it in bigger ways, like the ceremony story I related above. Either way, we need to be intentional about it. We need to show our sons how a wife should be treated, and we need to show our daughters how they should expect to be treated when they become wives. The best way to do this is to have an attitude of gratitude toward our wives at all times.

GamePlan

- As you correct your children, do you include affirmation? How can you be that tough, but encouraging, voice that inspires them to pursue excellence?

- Affirm your wife often in word and deed. Tell her she is a great mom, that you appreciate and respect her relationship with the Lord, and how she makes you a better man.

- Then model for others how great you think your wife is. Praise her in front of your children and your friends.

5

Kill the "Big S"

I have represented several players who have played alongside wide receiver Terrell Owens (T.O.), who is not known in the league for being selfless. These players say that everything T.O. does is geared toward drawing attention to himself. In January 2008, the Cowboys suffered a narrow playoff loss to the New York Giants. Tony Romo was catching a lot of heat for his play—and for a trip to Mexico he had taken during the bye week prior to the game with then-girlfriend Jessica Simpson. T.O. burst into tears in a post-game press conference in defense of his quarterback, but most players—including many of his teammates—rolled their eyes; they couldn't help but feel it was a show—an act intended to shine the spotlight on T.O. Personally, I don't know if he was being sincere or not. That's the problem with repeated selfish behavior. It casts a doubt on your intentions.

Conversely, Billy Bajema, a tight end for the Baltimore Ravens, has a reputation for being *unselfish*. In Billy's second year in the NFL, I attended the Senior Bowl and ran into the offensive line coach from San Francisco, where Billy had been drafted. He told me that Billy was one of the most well-respected guys on their team. "If I were walking down a dark alley," the coach said, "he's the guy I'd want next to me. He's all about the team and he'd never leave your side."

As a sports agent, I get to see the inner workings of NFL franchises. I observe many leaders, from owners to GMs to head coaches and even the position coaches. I see directors of player personnel and directors of college scouting. I see leaders of position groups and QBs who lead their teams. In almost every case, the teams with the best leadership are the teams that are the most successful, even if the on-field talent isn't the best.

The teams that struggle every year usually have something glaring in common: ineffective leadership. And the common thread among ineffective leaders is selfishness. When the GM is primarily concerned with who gets the credit, or an owner is worried more about the bottom line than putting a competitive team on the field, it shows. Selfishness is an illness that causes us to make terrible decisions and to rationalize reality away. It leads to more heartache than anything else in the world. I suffer from it, you suffer from it, and so does everyone else. The key question is: *Can we overcome it?* Can we get control of it? Can we stop letting it rule over us? It doesn't matter what the relationship is—selfishness can ruin it. The opposite is equally true. In fact, the number one statement I hear from NFL general managers about a player they feel they can't do without or a player they are particularly interested in signing is, "He is so unselfish."

Jared Cook is a tight end who was drafted by the Tennessee Titans in 2009. At the end of 2011, Jared was coming off his best season and was heading into his contract year. But instead of focusing on himself, and the money he could make as a free agent, and the fame that comes with personal success, Jared focused on winning games and making sure everyone got their share of the glory. Because Jared had been underutilized for the previous two seasons, his 2012 season was another letdown. But he kept going to work and striving for team success. He just kept showing up and working hard, trusting that it would pay off. And pay off it did. Jared was reunited with his former head coach, Jeff Fisher, at the St. Louis Rams. He was also rewarded handsomely with a contract that makes him the fifth-highest-paid TE in the NFL, with the third most guaranteed money.

Selflessness and selfishness are both matters of the heart. Matthew 6:21 says, "Where your treasure is, there your heart will be also." Most of us think of that verse in terms of finances, but if we treasure our families above all else, that is where our heart will be. Selfishness keeps us from those we love when we treasure our jobs, our friendships or our hobbies more than our families. It reflects our desire to serve ourselves rather than serve others. I call it *feeding the flesh*. We treat the symptoms, but not the underlying issue. We see this kind of approach all the time. When people have a problem sleeping, we give them sleeping pills. This may put them to sleep, but it does not address the deeper issue. Whatever it is that is making it hard to sleep is still there.

Selfishness is often easiest to see in kids. It is so pronounced. Kids struggle to say no to their selfish desires because, well, they are just kids. But oftentimes it becomes clear to me that just as I can so easily see selfishness in my kids, God sees the same thing in me. I chase my dreams and the things I like and want without even consulting Him. Or worse, perhaps, I consult Him without *listening* to Him. My parents did a great job of teaching me about selfishness. They also did a great job of showing me and my sister the joys of doing things for others. (She did a better job of learning the lesson, but that's a whole different story!) To be effective parents, we must teach our kids not only the destruction that selfishness can cause, but also the joys of selfless serving. More important, we must model these truths for them.

I used to be addicted to golf. Seriously. I have made some bad decisions about how to use my time based on my desire to get a round of golf in. I have rationalized playing golf versus being responsible. Now, golf is not a bad habit. Neither is fishing, hunting, going to movies, or a host of other pastimes. But when we put our desire to do those things above our families, our jobs, our friends, our spiritual lives or any other responsibility, we run into problems.

I admit I have rationalized going to play golf when I had important work to do. I have left my wife with all the responsibilities at home because I figured out how to slip off to the golf course. I have used the "I work hard and need this to unwind and get my frustrations out" defense so many times I bet my family can now predict when it's about to come out of my mouth. How about the "golf is cheaper than therapy" excuse? I have worn that one out too. And it's not like my wife minds that I play golf; she totally understands and is cool with it 999 times out of 1,000. It's just that one time when she needs me and I can't force myself to give up what I want that it is an issue. It finally dawned on me that I needed to refocus and reset my priorities. So, I actually dropped my club membership and now only play on occasion, so I can focus on my business and my family.

I know a lot of people who love to hunt. They would rather be outside in the freezing cold, just sitting there waiting for a big buck to wander up to the feeder for a snack so they can whack him, than doing anything else. I have to admit, I don't get it, but I know a lot of people who are into it. There is nothing evil about wanting to get outdoors, enjoy nature, and teach their kids about things they could never learn in a classroom. But many of the hunters I know will blow off significant obligations just so they can go hunting. They may drag a son or daughter along and call it "bonding with the children." Does that sound familiar? If this is hitting close to home, don't be mad at me; I have already confessed my issues. This is one of those things that are between you and the Lord. It is something you have to be totally honest with yourself (and Him) about.

So what's the answer? First of all, consider the apostle Paul's instruction: "I say to everyone among you not to think of himself more highly than he ought to think" (Rom. 12:3). Paul exhorted his audience to offer themselves as living sacrifices, and then he spoke about all of us being connected as the Body of Christ. After you've thought about yourself in relation to others, find a way to put your selfishness out in the open. Talk to your family about it. Let them know that this is something everyone deals with, including you. So often we feel like we have to hide our imperfections from our wives and kids. Like they don't already know we aren't perfect!

Finally, make serving one another and serving others outside of your home a priority. First Peter 4:10 talks about using the gifts God has given us to serve one another. Make service a part of your family culture. Teach your kids how to serve others and how to graciously accept being served. To take away someone else's joy of serving you is a form of selfishness.

When I was in the ninth grade, my mother taught me a valuable lesson. My grandmother kept driving to Dallas from Ft. Worth to watch me play soccer, and then she would take us all out to eat. I told her she didn't have to do this and stopped just short of telling her not to come to my next game. I just felt bad that she was going to all this trouble. My mother taught me that we should never take away another person's joy of giving. My grandmother loved to watch me play and loved taking us out to eat. She died while I was still young. I could have taken away an activity she loved, but thanks to my mom I learned to simply be grateful. Allowing my grandmother the ability to be unselfish was an act of unselfishness too. Selfishness is easy; it comes naturally to most everyone. Selflessness is a trait that is usually acquired through practice and by adjusting our hearts to look outward more and inward less—as modeled by Billy Bajema, Jared Cook and my grandmother.

GamePlan

- Facilitate a family discussion about selfishness. Let everyone share how selfish actions have hurt their feelings, and encourage them to discuss how some of their own actions can be selfish. Identify specific ways being unselfish benefits your family team.

- What blessings come from serving and developing a servant's heart? Demonstrate this principle by serving your own family, and brainstorm ways that you can serve others together.

- Find a place to serve the community as a family. A servant's heart usually needs to be developed. Put your team through its paces by serving together!

6

Act Right
Because It's Right

In 1993, Buddy Ryan was the defensive coordinator of the Houston Oilers, and Kevin Gilbride was the offensive coordinator. Ryan was known for having a great defensive mind, but he didn't seem to like Gilbride's pass-happy offensive scheme. All week, in their meetings discussing that week's game plan, it has been rumored that Ryan had repeatedly told Gilbride that the pass-pass-pass offense was putting undue pressure on his defense. The frequent three-and-out possessions were not allowing the defense to get rested, and that was causing them to underperform. So when Gilbride called a play that ended in an Oiler interception, Ryan decided to exact justice. He walked straight up to Gilbride, on the sidelines, and punched him in the face. Was Ryan concerned about the team, or about how his unit played? I don't know his motives, but his actions were caught on TV and were replayed over and over. The incident looked a whole lot like my kids in their playroom.

This was not just a failure of self-control, but a failure to commit to what was right for its own sake. One of the principles I teach my children is: "We all should act right *because* it's right." If doing to another what you'd want them to do to you is the *golden rule*, then this is the golden rule to the second power. Learning to own your own actions and behave well, regardless of how someone else treats you, is essential. One of the keys to being a winning family is learning not to let others' poor behavior determine your own.

When something is right, it's right. There is no need to debate whether you should do what is right. If the guy in front of you at the grocery store drops a $20 bill and doesn't realize it, you pick it up, stop him, and give it back. It's the right thing to do. I tell my boys to act right because it's right—end of story. There is no need to discuss it. In an effort to boil this principle down into something they could hold onto, I coined the phrase "Behavior Responsibility." The definition of Behavior Responsibility is as follows:

> You are responsible for your own behavior. You are not responsible for anyone else's behavior, and their behavior does not dictate how you behave.

You do the right thing, regardless of how anybody else decides to behave, because it's the right thing to do.

My boys are playing basketball. As my younger son drives the lane, his older brother pushes him and sends him skidding across the driveway. The younger boy gets up and throws his brother's brand-new Nike basketball up into the highest part of the monster oak tree in our backyard. So my older son punches him in the face. You are probably laughing right now, as I am, even though I actually saw this play out. We are each responsible for our own behavior, regardless of how other people behave. It is a form of accountability. I wish more people put it into practice more often, including my children.

In our me-first world (the finger is pointing at me now too), we see more and more that people are okay with retribution. A guy pulls into a parking place someone else was waiting on, so the other guy takes his key and scratches the paint down the side of the first guy's car. That'll show him. A lot of people will say that guy got what he deserved. It is almost acceptable. "What goes around comes around." In the Bible, God says, "Vengeance is mine" (Rom. 12:19). But people seeking vengeance against one another is happening everywhere—in the world, in the church, in the home. A husband isn't getting the emotional or physical attention he wants or thinks he deserves, so he turns to someone else. A wife feels she is underappreciated for all she does, so she strikes up an unhealthy relationship with another man. The pastor isn't getting the support he wants from a member of his church, so he shuts him out. Somebody cuts you off on the freeway and, for a moment, it becomes your life's mission to make that person pay. The wheel goes round and round.

Have you experienced your kids running in the room, one of them crying and screaming at the top of his lungs, "She kicked me," while the other one hollers, "He hit me first"? I was at a friend's house once, watching a scene like that unfold. I am embarrassed to admit that it made me laugh—but it was only because I had seen the same thing at home. My friend has three daughters. The youngest went into her oldest sister's room and came out wearing her sister's favorite earrings. The oldest sister screamed at her to take them off, and then the chase was on. The youngest flew out of the back door, followed closely by her furious sister. As she slowed to round the corner of the pool, her sister caught up and pushed her into the pool. Sitting on the side of the pool and laughing hysterically, the older sister did not notice that her younger sister was not laughing. Having just fixed her hair, and now waiting on her friends to pick her up, she did not see the humor in the situation. Getting out of the pool soaking wet, hair hanging down, and make-up streaking down her face, she jumped on top of her sister and started throwing punches and pulling hair.

Do you remember that this all started with a simple modeling of a pair of earrings?

This is a somewhat extreme example. But is it really that different from what we find between a husband and wife, or co-workers, or even drivers on the freeway? If everyone would extend half as much grace as they wish to receive and would adhere to Behavior Responsibility, the world would have no divorce, no war, and no need for police. I know that is not a realistic expectation for our world, but we can certainly work toward that goal in our homes. We can each choose what's right at the office, at church and on the freeway. Add in a healthy dose of forgiveness and who knows what our families would look like! Have you ever seen the bumper sticker that reads, "If it's going to be, it starts with me"? That's unrealistic, you say? Only if you believe it is. When I was in high school, a successful businessman told me that enthusiasm is contagious, and so is the lack of it. The same thing goes for being responsible for our own behavior. The world's response to the challenge to do something *selfless* is, "You first." Our response, especially in our homes, should be, "Okay, *me* first."

The NFL is no different from our families or any other sector of society. I have seen a number of teams get torn apart by a lack of Behavior Responsibility. Sometimes it is the offense versus the defense. The offensive players are scoring like crazy, but the defense can't stop the other team. So the offensive players get in the faces of the defensive players. The defensive players turn around and start bad-mouthing the offensive players in the media. The offensive players then go to the head coach or the GM and attack the defensive players or even the defensive coaches. Teams with these types of issues do not find themselves playing for Super Bowls, and these types of players do not find themselves in Canton making speeches in gold blazers in front of busts of themselves. The best teams and the best players are responsible for their own behavior. They do not behave based upon how someone else treats them.

Behavior Responsibility is not rocket science. It is a simple principle. The reason it's hard to incorporate into our lives is that our nature is to protect ourselves in whatever way we can. One of the easiest ways to protect ourselves from another person's bad treatment of us is to treat them the same way, or worse. But this only perpetuates the problem.

For example, maybe in the division of duties to keep your household running smoothly, your wife has agreed to prepare dinner most nights. Perhaps you would like to have a homemade dinner whenever possible, but your wife has grown accustomed to picking up dinner at a restaurant or putting together some of the easy-to-make store-bought meals. To get back at her, you might respond by withholding affection or not doing the dishes as you agreed to do when she does the cooking. That is what normally happens. You do *this* so I'll do *that*. It sounds childish and silly, and it is, but if you're honest with yourself, you will probably be able to find a couple of instances in which you have done this. Our spouses do it too. Maybe she likes the yard to be kept up, but although you agreed that this falls in your area of household responsibilities, you don't care if it goes an extra week without being mowed. So she becomes a little cool to you. You say, "Fine," and instead of hanging out with her on Saturday, you go golfing. Get the picture? It is silly and can easily lead to a downward spiral. Fortunately, there's a way to nip this in the bud. Open communication and implementing Behavior Responsibility will resolve most of your issues before they become major problems.

GamePlan

- Review the Behavior Responsibility principle with your family, including your wife. Admit your struggles in this area and invite your family members to share areas as well. Make this term a common phrase in your home.

- Identify specific situations where you tend to behave poorly towards your family. Determine better ways to respond when those situations arise.

- Make a commitment to practice Behavior Responsibility outside of the home. List specific areas where you want to improve. Share your experiences, good and bad, with your family. Encourage one another to behave well, even when friends, co-workers or teammates don't.

7

When Injured, Stop the Bleeding

One of my clients (we'll call him "Joe Smith") was having trouble coming down from the high of game day and was also dealing with the pain of multiple collisions that had had the force of two locomotives hitting head-on at full speed. So Joe started self-medicating. It began with a few beers but escalated to prescription drugs and more alcohol. It became harder and harder for Joe to get the edge off, creating a cycle that soon affected every aspect of his life. At first it wasn't that noticeable, but Joe's decline continued to intensify each week, until I received a phone call from Joe's wife. She was frantic. Joe's BMW was in a ditch at the entrance to their subdivision. He couldn't distinguish the pain of the previous game from the pain of the wreck.

Playing in the NFL is not at all what it looks like to the average fan. Fans show up on game day and see the players trot out onto the field in their neatly appointed uniforms. Their shiny helmets hide not only the players' faces but also the pain on those faces. Players are identified by numbers, positions, stats and accomplishments. The literal blood, sweat and tears that come along with preparing for a game, a season or a career are not visible to the public. When the players are in front of the camera, all of the pain has been temporarily washed away, and either the joy of victory or the resolve to come back from defeat has been painted on their faces.

Even players who don't get a lot of time in front of the cameras experience the same grueling rhythm. Unless you are the starting QB or RB, you just shower, get dressed, and head home after the game. You can walk away from the stadium virtually unnoticed by most fans. When you get home, you ache everywhere and oftentimes can't sleep. The highs and lows are so extreme, it's like being on a roller coaster.

Players know that a good season can lead to a huge payday and a bad one can lead to losing a starting position and eventually getting pushed out of the league. A constant awareness of this reality breeds fear about what they will do if that happens. Game days are filled with incredible highs, spiked with adrenaline and excitement. Mondays are filled with pain and stiffness, joy or worry depending on the outcome of the previous day's events, and the beginning of another week's cycle of preparation for another Sunday afternoon battle. Is it a blessing to be in the NFL? Absolutely. Few players would tell you differently. But is there a cost? Again, absolutely.

In Joe's case, I was forced to take drastic actions. Enlisting the help of the team, and one teammate in particular, we staged an intervention. You see, Joe was spiraling out of control, and the more he descended into chaos, the harder it was to stop it. Thankfully, the story ended well. Joe regained control and got his life and his career back on track. But had we not been able to stop the bleeding, who knows what could have happened. Joe was *injured*. He was bleeding out. He didn't need a Band-Aid. He needed a tourniquet. The first step was to identify the problem and evaluate the severity—and then to take decisive, appropriate action.

It's the same in our homes. We need to identify the challenges before they get out of control. If you have a child who is struggling in school, sneaking out of the house at night, or experimenting with drugs or alcohol, you can't just say, "Kids will be kids," and wait for it to pass. If you and your wife are growing apart and fighting on a regular basis, you can't just chalk it up to a rough patch and wait for it to pass. If your weight and your cholesterol are rising steadily, you can't ignore the problem and hope it magically stops. The next thing you know, you're getting a call from the police or the hospital regarding your child. Or you're announcing to your wife, "I can't live like this anymore. I want a divorce." Or a routine doctor visit ends up in open-heart surgery. It's easy to put your head in the sand and hope things just work out. Sometimes they do—but that is the *exception*, not the rule.

It is critical for us as men and as leaders to meet challenges head-on, turning them into *events* and not *trends* in our homes. One phenomenon I've noticed is that the different parts of our lives are interconnected, and positive events in one area of our lives can sometimes lead to challenges in other areas of our lives. A promotion at work leads to deterioration in our health, or our relationships at home suffer because we are working longer hours and are under greater stress. But a second, related phenomenon I've seen is that positive events in one area can also lead to more *good* things, like financial health, more fulfillment and improved self-esteem. I call this second progression the Theory of Momentum. Positive events lead to more positive events, and challenges lead to more challenges in other areas of our lives.

Consider this example of negative momentum in which a marriage goes from healthy to hurting to bleeding:

- Date night with your wife gets skipped as life gets crowded.

- You and your wife become disconnected.

- The more disconnected you are emotionally, the more disconnected you become physically.

- The more disconnected you are physically, the less time you make for each other.

- The less time you make for each other, the less in-tune you are with your wife.

- The less in-tune you are with her, the less you know about what she needs from you.

- The less you know what she needs from you, the less effective a servant leader you are.

You get the picture.

Most dysfunctional marriages don't go from honeymoon to hemorrhage in one step. I suspect you've either seen this or experienced it. A relationship becomes fractured and the partners disconnect, sometimes without even realizing it, until they find themselves so far apart they don't feel like they can get back together. I have seen marriages fail from the simple fact that a couple becomes emotionally disconnected. They stop talking about real things, they stop enjoying each other's company, and they drift or even fly apart.

Sometimes it starts after having children, the very thing that should keep us connected. When we have one child, it's easy to co-parent; we just use the "double-team." Then we have another and we have to go "man to man." One of us is handling the demands of the older child while the other is handling the more needy younger child. There are more nights without sleep and less time for each other. We slowly go from husband and wife to roommates. When more kids are added to the mix, it takes great leadership and commitment to maintain a thriving husband-wife relationship. I have said many times that I do not know how a fourth or fifth child is even conceived. Who has the time?

Momentum can sneak up on you, slowly gaining speed and force. If you are going to push a car that isn't running, you start by rocking it. Then, once the tire rolls over once, you can get it going a little faster—and the more momentum you gain, the faster it goes and the less you have to push. Satan uses this method in our marriages. He rocks them a little to get them going in the wrong direction—slowly at first. Then, once they're rolling, he can push less, and things just go wrong faster and faster until our once-healthy relationships plummet off the cliff.

As men, we can be so focused on things far from our homes that we don't realize how out of touch we are with our families. I heard one woman say that her husband was the last person on earth she would have sex with. She said that because of the way he treated her, the thought of it made her sick. Can you imagine having your wife feel that way about you? You may think that it could never happen to you, but that is exactly what this guy thought. Sadly, it happens every day. I heard a wise older man say one time that he finally figured out that the more he helped around the house, the more interested his wife was in being passionate with him. He said he wished someone had told him sooner.

It's important to remember how interconnected all the aspects of our lives are. We can have positive momentum in some areas of our lives and be bleeding out in others. It's a lot to be responsible for, I know. But that is what you are called to, and God created and equipped you to do it. He gave you everything you need to be good at it. What momentum do you have in your home?

GamePlan

- Be more aware of each situation at home. Do not assume that everything is okay. Ask questions about how each person is doing and feeling, and identify what things are troubling them. Be sensitive to the "at home but a million miles away" syndrome.

- Stop the bleeding! Any time you see the momentum going in the wrong direction, take action quickly. Do not let frustration or anger get the best of you. Let the peace of God rule your heart (see Col. 3:15), even when you have to take difficult steps to address an issue.

- Turn it around. Remember, even one small push can get the momentum going in the other direction. You will need to humble yourself, get out of your comfort zone and be unselfish. Seeing the benefits of your efforts can take time, but when they come they will be life changing.

8

Stay in Step

One of the most beautiful examples of teamwork is the way players on an NFL offensive line work in concert with one another. When the ball flies out of the center's hands, it is almost like these giants are dancing; they have learned to stay in step with each other. One of my former clients, Kelvin Garmon, affectionately known as KG to his teammates, describes the O-line as a team within a team. They call themselves "The Unit." The Unit is usually made up of men from all different walks of life. They represent different races and nationalities, and they come from different socio-economic backgrounds. Some are fresh out of college, while others have plied their trade in the NFL for many years, but when they come together they move as one.

KG describes it like this:

A successful Unit spends a lot of time together off the field and out of the locker room. Players get to know each other's families and develop a bond that most position groups don't need. With this bond come respect, love and accountability. Getting to know a player who plays next to you gives you the comfort of knowing their dedication to the business. Feeding our families, paying bills and taking care of responsibilities are not only up to you. The man playing next to you can affect the Unit, which can affect each player's family. So being the weak link in the Unit is something you never want to be.[1]

Most O-line Units across the league meet on Thursday nights for the lineman dinner. (Can you imagine what that table looks like?!) This is where they fine-tune the calls they will make to one another during the game. This is the language of the Unit—one that only they understand, one that tells each member of the unit which way to move and how to keep the opponent out of their backfield and off their quarterback. KG notes:

> Some calls are related to certain players on defense, while others relate to blitzes or stunts we may see coming. But we always add a *dummy* call. A dummy call is something that you may have used against your opponent in a previous game. Knowing that defensive linemen aren't completely stupid, we change up the calls so they won't key in on our blocking schemes. This keeps defensive fronts from deciphering our code.[2]

What if you could get your family to buy in to some of these O-line principles? To understand how successful they could be if they would all come together as a unit versus operating as individuals? It isn't our nature as human beings to desire this type of synchronistic behavior. Your job, as a leader in your home, is to get the Unit in step.

This is the greatest leadership challenge I face. With two adolescent boys, it seems futile at times. Then, as if out of nowhere, my boys see the benefit of working together and, like magic, they get in step. Finding a common goal with benefits for all parties is a great way to teach this principle. For instance, KG's Unit was united by the desire to provide for their families. When I tell my boys we can go to the pool as soon as the yard work is done, they have a tendency to work towards the common goal. One word of encouragement here: It isn't always going to look like it's working. Your kids are still kids! It may feel as though nothing is sinking in. Don't get frustrated; just be consistent with the message of unity. Mark 3:25 puts it like this: "If a house is divided against itself, that house will not be able to stand."

There are a few visible characteristics of a team whose members are in step with one another:

- Members pick their teammates up when they fall.
- They encourage instead of complain.
- They seek resolution without hurting other team members.
- They treat one another with respect.

A great example of this in my life has been in my relationship with my business partner, Craig Domann. We have been partners for over 20 years. We have had our share of disagreements and conflicts but, with respect, each of us has purposed to put the other's interests first. When issues have arisen, we've considered each other's point of view and talked it out. Craig has been a great partner and a great friend. He is a confidant for his players, giving them great advice that equips them to be highly successful. In the words of KG, our Unit has been built on "love, respect and accountability."

One of the most consistent traits I have seen from every winning Super Bowl team is strong team unity. The successful team includes 53 players, 12 to 14 coaches, dozens of equipment guys, trainers and doctors, front office executives and other business operations personnel working towards a common goal and staying in step. When a group of people pulls together for a common cause, with total commitment, amazing things can be accomplished. I say it often: The teams that pick at the top of each round, and the ones that pick at the end, are usually in those positions because of their leadership. Fractions within a group cause leaks in productivity.

I've heard that if you take the materials needed to create four one-gallon containers, and use those same materials to make *one* container, you can create a receptacle that will hold *six* gallons. That is the power of team. Michael Jordan, arguably the best basketball player of all time, was told by University of North Carolina head coach Dean Smith his freshman year, "If you can't pass, you can't play." Coach Smith knew that Jordan was a highly skilled player capable of great individual play *and* one who needed to understand that he was one of five players on the court. The lesson must have sunk in. After winning several NBA Championships, Jordan was quoted as saying, "Talent wins games, but teamwork wins championships."

One of the most interesting phenomena associated with team building is how going through a difficult situation together makes you closer. We see this happen on all kinds of teams all the time. Athletes striving for a championship work their tails off in extreme conditions. Army buddies go through life-threatening situations and come out with an unexplainable bond. Fraternities use this theory by making members pledge together. When you go through pain together, you come out closer. It is a bonding agent.

So how can you get brothers and sisters to stay in step and treat one another with respect? I'm not recommending hazing or boot camp, but sharing challenging situations *can* help them grow closer. Giving siblings joint projects and rewarding teamwork is a great way to help them get in step. Don't tell them how to do it; let them figure it out and let the reward be great. Kids are smart. We need to let them make some decisions, good and bad, so they can learn from their choices. Too many of us are shielding and coddling our kids, thereby depriving them of great learning experiences. Allowing them to tackle challenges, while offering support, builds team unity. If a bunch of immature college kids can figure out how to build unity among pledges, can't we do the same in our homes? Noted authors of *Creating the High-Performance Team*, Steve Buchholz and Thomas Roth, put it this way: "Wearing the same shirts doesn't make you a team."[3] You've given your family the same jersey; now make them a team.

GamePlan

- Take the reins. Team unity requires a strong leader. Seek counsel and support from a leader you respect and who does a good job of fostering unity and cooperation in his family.

- Develop your own leadership style. Tony Dungy and Tom Landry had similar leadership styles. Bill Parcells had a totally different style. Yet all three men won Super

Bowls and have the respect of those who have played for them. Develop a style that works best for you and with your team, and use it.

- Be intentional. Look for and even create opportunities to teach your family the benefits of working as a team. Come up with projects that require collaborative planning and effort. Reward your kids for sticking up for one another. Model this behavior by cooperating with your wife.

- Don't over-coach. Allow your family members to make decisions—and learn the hard lessons that come from making mistakes.

- Don't shield your family. If you are going through a tough time, let them know. So often we don't let our wives in on things that are troubling us because of pride or because we just don't want them to worry. Use common sense here, but remember that if you go through a tough time as a family, you will be closer for it!

Notes

1. Personal correspondence from Kelvin Garmon. Used by permission All rights reserved.
2. Ibid.
3. Steve Buchholz and Thomas Roth, *Creating the High-Performance Team* (Hoboken, NJ: John Wiley and Sons, 1987), p. 1.

9

Check Your Baggage

Robin "Big Cat" Jones played defensive end for Baylor University from 1988 to 1992, earning All-American third-team honors as a senior. His nickname was "Big Cat" because he was a massive man with lightning-fast reflexes. Robin played next to first-team All-American Santana Dotson as well as with a number of other highly touted players, including James Francis and Robert Blackmon. Robin was drafted by the Atlanta Falcons in the 1992 NFL Draft but injured his knee in training camp and never had the opportunity to prove he could make it on football's biggest stage. Robin was a young man who was used to overcoming adversity. He did not grow up in an affluent home. He would often quote the saying, "I once felt bad 'cuz I had no shoes and then I met a man who had no feet." As that quotation indicates, Robin is almost always positive and his attitude is infectious. Today he has three kids and is a successful father and husband. Robin understands what the members of any team must learn: It is your attitude that determines your altitude.

We all have baggage. We accrue it in our younger years and later we haul it into our marriages and families. The most successful people are those who learn to deal with the baggage of their past and become stronger because of it. It's not what happens to us that sets our course in life; it's how we respond to what happens to us that makes all the difference. As Robin Jones demonstrated, attitude is the most important factor in success.

Have you heard the amazing story of the bumblebee? It is said that a bumblebee should not be able to fly. Its body shape and mass in relation to its wing size and shape are not aerodynamic at all—but the bumblebee doesn't know this, so it flies anyway. When you find yourself scraping the ground because you've lost altitude, the first thing you should check is your attitude. I tell players all the time that although they can't always control being the best player in a matchup, they *can* control their effort. The same can be said of your attitude.

I love the Nike commercial that shows scenes from various youth football practices and games. You can see, and almost smell, the sweat on these young players. You can feel the complete exhaustion of their young bodies and the aches and pains from the long, hot practices. The last scene is a coach addressing his team. He says, "Men, let me assure you of one thing: The man who thinks he can and the man who thinks he can't are both right." I believe this.

I always tell my boys that I don't want to hear any "Yeah, buts." When I say one of them should have given more effort to studying, he may be tempted to reply, "Yeah, but . . ." I don't care what comes after a "Yeah, but"; it's never pertinent. My kids are not alone in this tendency; I have to force the attitude adjustment on myself sometimes.

You set the attitude of your household. Just as Robin's attitude is infectious, so too is yours—whether good or bad. It's the same at my house. If I'm not careful, I can let a tough day *I've* had turn my home into a tough place. I arrive home and the kids are getting along, my wife has not had a stressful day, and things are calm. Next thing you know, everyone's in a bad mood and frustrated with everyone else. Has this ever happened to you? Have you projected the stress of your day and your situation onto your family?

Or maybe you've had a perfectly good day—but then you walk in the front door and the kids are fighting and your wife is stressed out. She gives you that "what took you so long to get home?" look. You only have a moment to make a decision. Do you take on the stress of your household or do you change it? Do you get the kids under control and ask your wife if you can help with dinner? Or even offer to take the crew out for dinner? I can hear the objections already: *But I have been at work all day and I have stress that puts the home stress to shame. I need to be able to come home and have some peace, some dinner and a little TLC from my wife and kids.* Well, too bad! Nobody said that being a leader was going to be easy. Now don't get me wrong: If every night is like that, you may need to consider a more comprehensive overhaul. But if it's just a bad day, you have the opportunity to take a load off of everyone else's shoulders simply by having a positive attitude about the situation.

Maybe your wife loves to cook and is an excellent housekeeper. Maybe she has the kids fed, bathed and ready for bed every night without your assistance. Maybe she has ensured that they have their homework done and their teeth brushed, and they spend the rest of the evening quietly playing together. If this is the case, you may have married a Stepford wife! I'm just kidding, but the "perfect family" scenario is not the reality in most of the homes I know. What *is* the norm is coming into your home and dealing with what's actually happening, good or bad. *How* you deal with those things will set the tone for your family.

Ephesians 6:4 says, "Fathers, do not provoke your children to anger, but bring them up in the discipline and instruction of the Lord." It's our responsibility as leaders to create a positive environment in our homes. I am a naturally upbeat and positive person. I believe my parents contributed to that, both through my DNA and by their own dispositions. I have read many books by experts on positive mental attitude, as well.

God makes it clear how essential it is to have a positive mental attitude. He said in Proverbs 23:7, "As he thinks in his heart, so is he" (*NKJV*). He also gives us the ability to develop that attitude, even if it doesn't come naturally. There are some small ways we can adjust our attitudes that will make a big difference. Understand, as leaders of our households, we are responsible for a large portion of the attitude in our homes. I have a friend who calls himself a "realist." I call him a pessimist, and he is probably somewhere in between. While he may be willing to see the glass as half-full versus half-empty, he's quick to point out it *isn't* all the way full or even three-fourths full. You don't need to try to be something you are not, and you certainly don't have to be the second coming of optimist Zig Ziglar, but notice the perspective you're bringing to situations. Remember that how you view life is rubbing off on your wife, your kids, and everyone else you come in contact with.

There is a powerful story I heard about twin boys who grew up in an abusive, alcoholic home. Their father was a big man who liked to drink. He got filthy drunk every night, couldn't hold a job, and was verbally and even physically abusive to the boys and their mother. This man did not provide for his family and, when the boys were around 13 years old, child protective services removed them from the home. A researcher somehow found both boys when they were adults and interviewed them for his study. They had not been in contact for many years, and neither was aware of the other's situation. One of the brothers was living in a halfway house. He had been in and out of jail. He had three failed marriages, had two children with whom he had no relationship, and was in his fourth attempt at rehab.

The other brother became a successful businessman. He had launched and sold several companies. He was the outstanding father of three kids and was adored by his wife. He was involved in the community and had started a homeless shelter that catered to alcoholic men who had not been able to adjust to being a father or husband. He was the chairman of several charities and was a strong leader at his church.

Both men were asked the same question: "To what do you attribute your current position in life?" The interesting thing is that they both had the same answer: "With a father like mine, what else would you expect?"

How you and I look at our lives and our situations will determine how we handle the trials that will undoubtedly come our way. Do we look at the "successful" people in our world and think how lucky they are and how we got a bad deal in life? Do we inadvertently teach our children that they should expect others to get preferential treatment because that has been our experience in life?

The flipside is equally powerful. If you could ensure that your wife and kids feel as though they can do anything, wouldn't you do that for them? Wouldn't you want them to feel that they could conquer the world? We can teach our families that no matter how good or bad things get in our lives, there is always someone who has it better and someone who has it worse. We will get preferential treatment in some instances, and we will get the short end of the stick in others. That's life. It's not what happens to us in life that matters; it is how we react to what happens to us that will define who we are.

GamePlan

- Check yourself. Take a good, hard, honest look at where you are in the attitude department. We may start the day singing and end it crying. I have a motto that helps me: *There are no problems, only opportunities*. But the fact is, sometimes the opportunities seem overwhelming. Are you ready for anything? Can you trust that God has a plan for you? How can God help you gain a more positive outlook on life?

- Check your output. This is the vibe you are putting off to everyone else. If you're not sure how you're coming across, ask the people close to you for their insight. Commit to being encouraging. Figure out who needs a hug, who needs a word of exhortation, and who needs a laugh. You'll find that if you are the giver of these things, you will benefit as well.

- Sow some seeds. Make a commitment to take a more positive approach to everyone in your life. Come up with specific steps you can take to turn any problem into an opportunity. You will be amazed by the effects of your shift in attitude.

- Make mid-course corrections. If you catch yourself slipping into old negative habits, recognize it and fix it. Ask your wife, your kids, or others close to you to help you watch for attitude problems.

- Be a coach. Talk to your family about how to have a positive outlook. How can you encourage each other to be more positive? If you don't come by this naturally, don't be discouraged. It will be a good bonding exercise for you to work on this together.

10

Establish Trust

Kevin Mathis played at a small college, Texas A&M Commerce (previously known as East Texas State University). Kevin was from Gainesville, Texas, which is located about 60 miles north of Dallas. Gainsville is a small town, and East Texas State was a small school not known for producing NFL players. However, Kevin was a gifted player and had one quite remarkable trait: speed.

When I met Kevin, I immediately noticed something that gave me confidence in him. He was not loud and boisterous, as some cornerbacks are known to be, and he was not cocky. He had a quiet assurance that drew me to him. I signed Kevin as a client and immediately started the preparation process to get him noticed by the NFL. He signed a free agent contract with the Dallas Cowboys and went to training camp. Although the NFL can be "too big" for some players from small towns and small colleges, that was not the case with Kevin. He did go through an adjustment period, though. Division I-AA football was worlds apart from the NFL. I shared a secret with Kevin early on that would later prove to be vital. I told him that no matter how skilled he was, he had to gain the trust of his coaches and the veteran players before he would get any significant playing time.

In Kevin's first NFL game, he had two interceptions and he blocked a punt that was recovered for a touchdown. To the outside world, and by all accounts in the media, it appeared that Kevin was well on his way to not just making the team but also becoming a major part of the Cowboys defense. Kevin remembered what we had talked about, and he made it a point to get close to Deion Sanders. After that first game, Kevin didn't go around acting like he "had arrived." He talked to Deion about the mistakes he had made, about how he could better recognize routes, and about how he could improve his technique. Because of Kevin's humility and his eagerness to learn and improve, Sanders knew the rookie he called "little fella" was going to be good—really good. Kevin had gained the future Hall of Famer's trust. And because Deion trusted him, the coaches and the other vets began to trust him too. Kevin went on to have an outstanding career, playing for the Cowboys, Saints and Falcons. He gained a reputation as someone who cared for his teammates. He made everyone around him better and was like a coach on the field. All of this was achieved because he was worthy of the trust his teammates gave him—not just on the field, but off of it as well.

Trust is a topic that comes up in every relationship. As an agent for NFL players, coaches and front office personnel, it is the first obstacle I have to overcome. When I meet a college football player for the first time, I usually ask him what he is looking for in an agent. Invariably the player replies, "Trust." There is no place that requires more trust than your home. Obviously, your marriage will never be vibrant without it, and your relationship with your kids cannot be great without it, either.

The old adage is true: *Trust is earned, not given.* I have heard many people say that they choose to trust others until they are given a reason not to. I'd counter that by suggesting that you can't really trust people until they earn it. Those who want your trust need to do something to show that they are trust*worthy*.

Now, a common misconception about trust is that you have to be perfect to be trustworthy. Many times we perpetuate this misconception: People don't do what they say they are going to do, we feel let down, and we say we can no longer trust them. We withhold our trust. The fact is that no one is perfect. If you are the one who has let somebody down, you have a responsibility to be accountable. If someone lets *you* down, and they admit it and apologize, that is a trust-building action. Have reasonable expectations for people and they will probably have the same for you. We need to teach our families how to *earn* trust, how to *give* it, and the standards to which we can reasonably hold ourselves and others.

Our family usually goes to our local high school football games on Friday nights in the fall. Our boys love to go, even though they don't ever watch the game. They hang out with their friends in the end zone area. Eli and his buddies still throw the football around and play. Jake and his friends have graduated to the "stand around and talk" phase—with girls, if at all possible. During one game, Jake came and sat by his mom and me midway through the game, something that is unheard of for a teenage boy. I was sure he needed money, but I liked his method of going about getting it, so I let him roll with it. After a few minutes had passed without any mention of money, I inquired, "What are you doing here?" Jake laughed and said he just wanted to watch a little of the game. I guess he realized that my puzzled look meant I needed some further clarification. He admitted that his friends' conversation had gone to a place he was not comfortable with, so he had slipped away to come sit with us. This was a huge trust-building event for us. He assured me that his friends weren't up to anything crazy, but he just felt he would be better served by removing himself from the conversation. I made a big deal of his actions and reaffirmed how what he did allows me to trust him more and therefore give him more freedoms.

Trust issues can only be resolved when we face them and deal with them. I frequently encounter men and women who say they don't trust their spouses but won't talk to them about it. It's like they are waiting for trust to magically happen some day. It's the same with our kids, our friends and our business relationships. If you feel that someone doesn't trust you, talk to that person and find out why; you may discover that it isn't the case at all, or you might have your eyes opened to something you need to address in your own life. If you don't trust someone close to you, be honest with that person about how you feel he or she let you down. The relationship will be healthier because of it. A lack of trust is a huge emotional and physical drain. It will wear you out.

When we consider trust between husbands and wives, the most common concern is about fidelity. And while this is of course critical, it's not the end-all when it comes to trust in a marriage. There are a number of areas where trust is critical:

1. Fidelity
2. Finances
3. Your word
4. Commitment to the new family unit
5. Protection
6. Leadership

Fidelity

The importance of being faithful to your spouse goes without saying. Fidelity is a vow you made on your wedding day. It is a centerpiece of your marriage that is paramount to enjoying a healthy relationship with your wife. The Bible speaks of sexual sin as being worse than others because it is sin against one's own body. I doubt there are many men reading this book who would disagree with the idea that fidelity is important. However, some might not recognize that emotional fidelity is just as critical as physical fidelity. I'm astonished by the number of men (and women) who would never dream of committing physical adultery but commit emotional adultery without even thinking about it.

Emotional adultery is sharing with another woman any emotional issue that should be reserved for your wife. This includes discussing any problems in your marriage or things you don't like about your wife. I once had a guy tell me he used to talk about sex with a woman at work; he said she was just a friend. *Are you kidding me?!* Not cool, dude. It is emotional adultery. Even if you aren't sharing your secrets with another woman, but she is sharing hers, it's still emotional adultery.

You need to be able to trust your wife in her commitment to fidelity, as well. I know of men who, for whatever reason (sometimes warranted and sometimes not), cannot seem to trust their wives in this area. They are super-jealous. If this is you and there was an incident that caused the lack of trust, you need to address it. If there are no reasons or incidents, you still need to address it! I know a man whose wife was married previously. She had an affair and her marriage broke up. He confided in me that he was jealous when it came to his wife and he didn't understand why. I told him that even though her infidelity was not within *their* relationship, he knew of it and couldn't help but have some questions. She was a different person now than she had been before and he knew this, but they still had a trust issue and they needed to deal with it.

Finances

Show your wife that you are a good steward of your family's finances. Prove to her and to your kids that you can manage the family income and pay the bills on time. She needs to trust that you will not go buy into a deer lease when you don't have your retirement or the kids' college educations paid for. If you do not feel qualified to handle the family finances, get some help. There are many excellent, affordable financial training programs out there. You can't go wrong with anything from Dave Ramsey.

Your Word

My dad taught me early on in life that my word was my bond. He said that if people didn't believe me when I told them something, then I was not going to get far in life. Your wife needs to trust that if you say you'll go get the kids at practice, stop for milk on the way home, and be back in time for dinner, you will do it. Remember the comment that nobody is perfect? It's true, so don't beat yourself up if there are times when you are unable to do what you said you would do. But make sure that not keeping your word is the exception, not the norm. Be accountable. The best way to teach your kids how to keep their word is to keep yours.

One key to being a man of your word is to avoid overpromising. If your son asks if you are going to be at his game and gives you those sweet eyes, don't say yes just because you don't want to hurt his feelings. Explain what is going on in your life that might prevent you from making it. Let him know that his game is important to you, but that you have other responsibilities that might keep you from it. If you tell him yes and then don't make it, that will be more damaging in the end. Little things, like being on time, count. Be a man of your word.

Commitment to the New Family Unit

You are probably wondering what I am talking about. Well, you know how at weddings we often hear talk about "leaving and cleaving"? The fact is, some men and women just *leave*. When we get married, we are meant to leave our old family units and form new ones. But it's odd, if you think about it, to grow up in a family and then leave it and start a new one. If we are loyal team members, and our old family units were close ones, it might be a little difficult.

It is usually a little harder for women to truly leave and cleave than it is for men. It took me 10 years to get my wife to stop calling her parents' house *her* house! We had kids, we had bought a house, and that was *our* house. Our parents will always be family, but they have to be #2, not #1B.

If we don't cleave, we are tempted to run "home" when something doesn't go just right in the new home. "Running home" might not be a physical flight—it could also be an emotional withdrawal. After we marry, our parents and their homes are no longer our default safe havens. If you or your wife consistently turn to your parents, instead of to each other, authentic trust is impossible. This will be a difficult issue for some men in leading their homes, but it can be overcome. How you handle this will depend on your wife's personality and the amount of trust you have established with her in other areas.

I have some friends who recently got married. They have a great Christ-centered marriage, but they also have a big wedge between them: His mother won't let go. She still treats him like he is her little baby. They have always been close, and he was a little older when he got married, so Momma had him longer than most. Consequently, she is having a hard time releasing him to cleave to his wife. My friend needs to show his bride that he is committed to their new family unit, but he is having a hard time doing so. His wife feels that he is (1) being a wimp, and (2) choosing his mother over her. She has a valid point. His mother is dictating what they do on holidays, manipulating him, and harming his relationship with his wife. My friend's wife cannot have a relationship with her mother-in-law because her husband is not handling the situation properly.

Protection

To protect one's home and family is a primal instinct. As the man of the house, we need to assure our wife and kids that we can and will do anything and everything to protect them. They need to know we will lay our lives down for them. Thankfully this doesn't mean we need to become body builders, martial arts experts, or proficient with guns and knives. It means our families need to trust that we will make good decisions that will not put them in harm's way. They need to know: *Dad's got this.*

Their trust in your ability and willingness to protect them will grow from the actions you take to protect their emotions and their spirits. Your family needs to know that you are behind them in all they do. Layne and I don't let our boys call female friends at school *girlfriends*. We have explained to them that they are not emotionally mature enough to even know what a girlfriend is or how to handle that kind of relationship yet. We have explained the pitfalls, and now they are beginning to see that we are protecting them. That builds trust.

Leadership

More than anything, we need to demonstrate to our families that they can trust our decision-making process—that we will lead them in a way that will be best for them, even if it doesn't seem like it at the time. Sometimes situations will arise in our lives that we can't control. But even in those times, our families need to be able to trust that we are going to make the right decisions for our family.

Great leaders include their families in the decision-making process. Because, as the leader of your family, you have the last say, it can be tempting to behave like a dictator! At the other end of the spectrum, I'm not suggesting that you let your eight-year-old veto a move and keep you from taking a new job in another city. But do give your family a voice and make them a part of the decision-making process. It will help you build trust as a leader.

In 2003, my wife and I decided to build on the property we had purchased in Salado, Texas, a small town in the Texas Hill Country where we would move with our then two- and four-year-old boys from Dallas. We took the boys down to see the land we had bought, showed them the school they would be going to, and took them to the creek in town where they would get to play. They bought into our dream of moving and felt involved. As we were finalizing the plans for our new home and preparing to sell our house in Dallas, my wife was diagnosed with rheumatoid arthritis. The ensuing months were terrible for her physically and for both of us emotionally. Needless to say, our lives were turned upside down. Because her pain was debilitating, making a major move seemed absurd. However, after spending time in prayer and giving it a lot of consideration, we made the decision, as a family, that we needed to move forward. Against the wishes of many friends and some family, we moved into a townhouse in Salado, built our house, and then moved once again into the new place. It was hard, but looking back it was the right thing to do and everybody was on board.

Trust is a huge topic and is one of the major building blocks of a family. Trust is one of the cornerstones of any relationship, and it is paramount for you to be an effective leader. Leading your family in a trustworthy manner is what will earn you your family's trust. The onus is on you.

GamePlan

- Determine areas in which you need to gain trust. Talk to your wife and ask her to share any areas in which she does not totally trust you. Understanding where there is a lack of trust is the first step. What can you do to show yourself as more trustworthy in these areas?

- Talk to your kids about the importance of trust. Are there times when they don't feel "safe" with you? If so, this could be a sign of a lack of trust on their part. If your kids are older, your conversation will be more direct. What steps can you take to help your kids have greater trust in you?

- Be open with your wife if there is an area where you do not trust her. Being honest allows you to work on it. Be constructive. What changes can each of you make that will help you trust her more fully?

- As appropriate to their ages, give your kids opportunities to earn your and your wife's trust. Where can they be given new responsibilities or privileges? Be clear about how this opportunity will build your trust.

11

Control the Pace

In 2007 I was introduced to the offensive coordinator of the Tulsa Golden Hurricane, Gus Malzahn, a former high school coach. I was impressed with his offensive philosophy and agreed to become his agent. In December 2008, Coach Malzahn was hired as the offensive coordinator at Auburn University, where he helped lead the Tigers to a national championship in 2010. He was successful because he ran a blazing-fast offense. While other coordinators were running 60 plays a game, Coach Malzahn was running 80 to 90 plays. His players were required to hand the ball to the referee after every reception so that the next play could start as quickly as possible.

His style was so maddening that opponents would "lose" their helmets so that the officials would stop the game until the players got their helmets back on. Some teams would coach their players to feign injury in order to slow the game down. These sneaky attempts to hinder Auburn's pace resulted in the NCAA implementing a new rule just to prevent such manipulation. Coach Malzahn has changed the way teams now play the game, and the trend in both college and professional football is a fast-paced offense. Coaches know that if a team can control the pace, they can control the game. The same is true in all of life. If you let life simply take its course, you'll be swept up in a no-huddle, fast-paced life—the kind that's marked by a lack of intentionality.

I graduated from Southern Methodist University in 1982 and moved into a duplex shortly thereafter. The owner of the building lived in the other half of the duplex. He owned a pharmacy and worked ridiculously long hours. One day I went out for a run and, as I finished up back at the front of the property, I saw an unusual sight. My landlord was pulling into the driveway and it was only nine o'clock at night—an early evening for him! Did I mention that I never saw him? I told him it was good to see him and, trying to be funny, I made a comment about him slacking off that day or something equally awkward. Not seeming to catch the humor, he mumbled, "You don't own your own business; your business owns you." At the time I passed it off as a well-rehearsed comeback to a poorly executed joke. I have since started my own business, and experience tells me that my neighbor was onto something. If you are not careful, "You don't live life; life lives you."

Time management used to be a concept; now it is a skill—a curriculum. There are 99,317 books on Amazon *alone* dedicated to time management. You can take courses at most major universities on time management skills. Life has a way of running our lives. Sounds funny but you know how true it is. I laugh at myself when I think about how many times I told my parents, during my college years, that I would love to come home and see them, but I was just too busy. And I went to school in the same town they lived in! I just thought I was busy.

Now that I have a wife and kids, and this business I started in 1990, I know what *busy* really means. The key for me as a husband and a father is establishing some guidelines with my family. There are certain areas that demand our time and must be addressed. Work is an obvious time bandit for all of us and is usually not optional. Ours is a big sports family, and my wife is right there with us. Both of our boys are in season in at least one sport all year long, and until recently, it had been two sports. We attend Baylor and SMU games, San Antonio Spurs games, and also our local high school sporting events. That doesn't even take into account the numerous games I attend in the course of my work as an agent. Free time is important to us, so we have set aside a reasonable amount of free time for each member of the family. Then we have date night, church activities, family time, and time for members of the extended family, such as grandparents, aunts and uncles. Before you know it, life is controlling our pace.

If you are like most people, you have to work. There is a growing sense in the workplace that our time belongs to our employers. I have many friends who work at NFL teams, and the time required by an NFL franchise is unbelievable. I have several friends who are NFL general managers and who know about my passion for helping men become more effective in their homes. One of them (let's call him "Robert") called me just the other day and asked me for the magic pill—the one that would allow him to be great at his job and great at home. I told him the truth: *There isn't one.*

Working for an NFL franchise is like what happened to an old man I met while on a recruiting trip out to West Texas. He said he had worked for a rancher for years, proclaiming his boss the greatest guy in the world. The owner of the ranch supposedly had told my new friend he only had to work half-days—and he didn't care which 12 hours it was! Sometimes you have to choose between a great job and a great family. I told Robert it wasn't *impossible* to be great at both, but he'd have to have an understanding owner and a budget for extra help. Another key ingredient to controlling the pace at work is the ability to delegate. Some can and some can't. What about you? Can you give a subordinate a task and leave the office? Do you have somebody to whom you can delegate?

If you are going to control the pace at work, you must set boundaries. Sometimes the only way to enforce the boundary is to find another job. I realize that may not be easy. But if you feel that you can't enforce the boundaries you need at your current job, it may be what you need to do. (By the way, I would suggest finding the new job before you leave the one you have!)

Controlling the pace also requires becoming a better time manager. Being efficient with the work you manage will help you protect the time you need for other areas of your life. More important, and this is my biggest issue, leave work at the office! Being a sports agent means being on-call all the time. I don't sleep with my cell under my pillow like some agents, but I do have to be available. I have a deal with my clients: *If you need me at an hour that is not a normal business hour, let me know and I'll respond. If it can wait, let me know that too, and I will respond in a reasonable amount of time.* I represent mature, responsible men, so this arrangement generally works well. I am glad to be there for my clients when they need me. I just don't want to be that guy who is at his kids' soccer game but is standing down the sideline on his cell—there physically but absent in spirit and mind.

If you have kids, you know the kinds of time strains their activities can create. There is schoolwork, special projects, dance, cheer, music, sports, scholastic competitions, and more. We are all sports fanatics in our family, so a great deal of our time is devoted to sports. I joke that I vetted my wife on the whole *love of sports* thing first, and she says she did the same! But even the fun events that we all enjoy can get out of control; before we know it, we are racing from one to the other, or splitting up with me taking one son to his game while my wife takes our other son to his. We meet back at the house, exhausted, not having been able to hang out as a family and enjoy one another's events. So one of the things we have done is limit the number of sports our boys play in a season. Your kids' sports or other activities can rule your life if you let them. Be aware so you can head this off before it becomes an issue. In my case, my wife is a great check-and-balance system for me. I would probably overdo it if she weren't there to rein me in sometimes.

If you are married and don't have children, I say enjoy each other and enjoy the quiet! Don't be in a hurry to add kids to the mix. Get to know each other and develop that strong bond that grows by spending quality time together. I mean *really* get to know each other—the great attributes and also the quirks. Before you have kids, learn how to manage your time with just one more person to put before yourself—your wife! Learn how to manage what you already have on your plate: the pursuit of your career, spending time with your wife, spending time with your friends, your church life, your sports interests, and more. Then start your family, if that is your desire.

Having children is the most awesome thing you will ever do together, but it can also be the greatest source of stress in your marriage. Make some decisions about how you want to bring your kids up before you have them! Talk about discipline, school, sports, church involvement, diaper changing, feeding, and whether or not your wife will continue to work outside the home.

Or perhaps you're heading toward the back end of the kid cycle and preparing to be empty nesters. Controlling the pace in this season also requires some work! Start looking ahead to what will fill the void that is created by the kids moving out, going to college, or starting their own families. Help establish a legacy with your kids, even if you didn't do a great job of it when they were younger.

Whatever stage of family life you are in, take a good look at your free time, time you spend with friends, and any other areas that are sources (or potential sources) of conflict in your home. Learn to control the pace now and you will be ready to control the pace with every change in your family structure.

GamePlan

- Start now! No matter what your situation is, plan your life rather than reacting to it. You will be better at everything you do if you are proactive with your time.

- Assess! List the areas of your life that are being neglected because you run out of time. If some of the items on your list are not essential, let those go. For the ones that are important, start thinking about how to carve out time to get to them.

- Act! Don't procrastinate. Adjust your work schedule. If your kids are stretched too thin, rein that in as well. Talk with them about using their time and how an out-of-control pace is detrimental to family life.

- Have a family activity each week where you don't watch TV. Play games, go on a bike ride, have a picnic at the park, whatever you can think of. Don't blaze through life without really connecting. Even when you are together, are you really connecting as a family, or are you running around and stressed all of the time?

12

Watch Your Words

Words are powerful. A coach's words can motivate a team to overcome a deficit. A quarterback's can set a cadence for a perfectly timed snap. But if used poorly, words can get a player ejected from a game or isolated on his team.

A client of mine (we'll call him "Jason") was a wide receiver at Southern State in Florida. Jason was excited to be playing Division I football. He had dreamed all his life of playing in college. Now, having made it this far, his ultimate goal of playing in the NFL was in view. Jason had been recruited by Southern State's offensive coordinator, Coach Williams. Coach Williams was not an overly imposing figure physically, but he commanded a room and his knowledge of football was inspiring. Coach Williams noticed Jason during his sophomore year. Jason had never played receiver but was quickly described as a natural. He became a starter and was second on the team in receptions and yards and led the team in touchdowns that year.

Jason describes the first letter he received from Coach Williams. Looking back it's apparent it was a form letter, but at the time, it was like gold. Jason loved the game, and pretty soon other schools took notice. Jason started getting more letters and phone calls from other coaches, and they began recruiting him. But Coach Williams had been the first. Jason eventually selected Southern State over several other colleges. When he took his official visit to State, he met the rest of the coaching staff, but it was in large group settings. They all seemed like good guys, passionate about winning and very motivating. The head coach, Coach Vickers, was a former NFL player. Jason remembered thinking that Coach Vickers might have been hit in the head a few too many times, but he laughed it off! When the game they had been brought in to witness went south, and State lost, Coach Vickers went on a rant during his address to the recruits. Again, Jason laughed it off. He would soon find out, though, that it wasn't funny.

During the middle of Jason's freshman season, a season that hadn't gone so well, Jason finally got the call to get in the game. The starter had pulled a hamstring, and Coach Vickers didn't like what he saw from the backup. Jason didn't care what the circumstances were that had led to him getting his number called; he was just glad to get some game time. After the first series, with live bullets flying, Jason discovered it was not so easy to run precise routes. A first-down run resulted in a 5-yard loss, so passes were called on second and third downs. On second down, Jason was supposed to run a 10-yard hitch, but tight coverage by the cornerback caused Jason to pull up at 8 yards. The pass sailed over his head and was nearly picked off. On third down, the play called for a combination route where Jason was the secondary target. But he did not run the exact route called for, resulting in another incompletion. Jason was hoping his mistake wouldn't be noticed.

As he jogged to the sideline, Coach Vickers made it clear that *it was noticed*. He grabbed Jason by the facemask and, in a mixture of profanity and spit, he made his point. Jason had been coached hard before, and was okay with that style, but there was something different about how Coach Vickers handled these types of situations. He made it personal. Over the course of the season, Vickers took more and more verbal shots at players. The team was having a decent season, but the morale of the players was spiraling downward. Jason wondered if he wanted to play college football anymore if it meant playing in that environment. Jason didn't quit, but he did enter the draft early as a junior, partially to remove himself from that environment. As for Coach Vickers, let's just leave it by saying that he's no longer the head coach at State.

We've all heard the old saying, "Sticks and stones may break my bones, but words will never hurt me." Though the adage has a catchy ring to it, it is not actually true. Our words do have great power—especially in the home. Coming from a spouse or a parent, words can hurt or heal, tear down or build up. In fact, the Bible is full of statements about the power of the tongue. If you think it isn't true, just take a barb from a friend or a spouse, or even worse a parent, and see how you feel. It's nice to say that words don't hurt us, but they can. It is how you and I were designed. Learn not to misuse words—or to avoid them altogether if you need to in certain situations. Begin to dismantle patterns of communication that use harmful words, and find ways to build your family up with instructive correction versus criticism. Your family will follow your lead. The way you communicate with your family is how they will communicate with one another.

There are numerous examples in the Bible of the father, as a person of authority, speaking blessings over his family. In the culture of the Old Testament, a father would give his oldest son his blessing. There are also examples of parents speaking curses over their families. When we speak positive affirmations over our families, we are speaking blessings over them; when we speak negative things over them, we are actually speaking a curse over them.

I heard a story about a mother who, in frustration, told her child, "You are always sick." Not surprisingly, her daughter continued to be sick a lot. If you are prone to bursts of anger that are laced with hurtful words, you need to know how damaging your words can be. If you are inclined to be sarcastic, as I am, be aware of the pain you can cause. We need to think before we speak. I know I am a pretty quick draw with my tongue. I am trying to slow it down a bit and allow my brain to get involved.

There are the obvious hurtful statements made in anger, but there are also statements that can cut in more subtle ways, wounding slowly and deeply: Telling a child that if he doesn't get better grades in school he'll end up digging ditches. Telling a child he won't be successful in life. Telling a girl she is dressed like a prostitute. Don't laugh—you would be surprised how often things like that are said without parents recognizing the weight their words carry. I have a friend who is known to call players on his eight-year-old son's sports team *girls* when they are playing soft. Not only is he disrespecting women—not a great example for young boys—but he is also damaging the psyche of those boys. Telling your wife, "You are just like your mother," in a derogatory way, can harm her at her core. Calling her a terrible cook—wrong on many levels—and then expecting her to become a good one is like putting water in your car's gas tank and expecting it to run.

It's important to make sure your kids understand the power of their words as well. If your child comes home with a bad grade, he or she might say, "I'm just stupid." Don't let that wide-ranging self-critical statement stand. Redirect the conversation by encouraging your child to say something more positive, specific and constructive. You could offer a few examples like, "Wow, I really blew that class," or "I made a mess of the test and it cost me; guess I'd better study harder next time." Don't allow your children to speak curses over themselves, even if it's done to temper your anger with them. Every time my wife and I are discussing something we disagree on, our youngest says, "Are you going to get divorced?" Maybe it's because he has friends who have divorced parents. We have told him and his brother many, many times that divorce is not an option in our house and that we will never get divorced. We have to tell him not to speak that over us or anybody else. I had a client who experienced a series of freak injuries. One time he said, "I'm guess I'm just one of those guys that's injury-prone." I encouraged him to take it back and say instead, "I'm not going to have any more of these injuries." Or in my case, I used to say jokingly, "You're killin' me," when someone would do something that didn't help my cause. My wife was quick to remind me that this was *not* what I needed to be speaking over my life!

Teach your kids corrective instruction versus harmful criticism, you and your wife leading by example. When there is a need for correction, address your family member's behavior rather than attacking him or her personally. If my son is behaving immaturely, I don't call him a baby—even though I may want to sometimes. Instead, I may point out that he is *behaving* like he did when he was much younger and ask him why he would behave in a manner that is not consistent with his age and character. I tell him that he is a mature, smart young man and ask him why he is not behaving that way. If your son is acting like a punk, don't call him a punk. Tell him, "You are a smart, funny, cool kid. Why would you say things a punk would say?" You have made your point, given him an encouraging and affirming word, and corrected the behavior. If you call your kids names, you are "tagging" them and those labels take root in their subconscious. You can actually program them to be exactly what you *don't* want them to be! I have to admit, I have not always been great at this. It is something I've had to work on.

Words spoken between spouses are equally important. If you have an issue with your wife, you have a choice: You can lash out and say harmful things or you can respond with kindness and compassion, get your point across, and not cause your spouse any unnecessary pain. Now, if you are like me, you can get overly excited and speak before you think. That goes for the quieter, snide comments as well as the high-volume, angry ones.

When we were growing up, my buddies and I used to hang out at a friend's house. We were sitting in his living room one summer evening, and his mom asked his dad, "Bill, how can I lose 10 ugly pounds fast?"

His dad responded, "Cut off your head." Now, he was kidding, and the joke still makes me laugh, but there is no telling how deep that wound went, not to mention the lesson he taught several young boys about how a husband is to treat a wife. Bill was a great guy and had a knack for making people laugh. He wasn't being mean to his wife, at least not on purpose. But he hadn't thought through how his words might affect her, so when a funny line came to his mind, he blurted it right out and disrespected her in the process.

It's interesting how certain situations bring out the worst in us. What do you do when your wife voices her displeasure after coming home to find you sitting on the couch, your dirty laundry on the floor, your shoes kicked off in the living room, and your water glass in the process of leaving a ring on the coffee table? Do you come back with a list of *her* shortcomings? It might sound something like this: "Well, if you care so much about this house, why did you leave the breakfast dishes in the sink all day and let the trash can overflow on the floor?"

To which, she might respond, "If you saw that those things needed to be done, why didn't you do them? I was the one who got the kids ready for school, made everyone's breakfast, including yours, and had to rush out to work after dropping off the kids."

Before we go any further, do you remember Behavior esponsibility? You see, it doesn't matter how she spoke to you; as the leader of your house, you have to set the example. So, regardless of how your wife initially communicated her frustration, your response should be something to the effect of, "Sorry, babe, you're right." Period! If you have a problem with the dishes in the sink, don't use her complaints as an open door to address your issues with her. Deal with those separately, without making cutting comments about her.

You might later say something like, "Honey, I came in the house and I saw the dishes in the sink and the trash spilling out on the floor, and I reacted by taking the attitude that if no one else cared about our home, why should I? It was an immature response and I was wrong for doing that."

To which she might very well say, "I am sorry I left that stuff; I knew it was going to wig you out. I should have taken the time to take care of it."

At which point you could say, "Well, I know you got up and got the kids ready for school, made our breakfast, made the kids' lunches, and flew out to get them to school and yourself to work. Why don't I get the trash and you get the dishes? After all, we're a team, right?"

Obviously, the conversation may not happen quite as smoothly as what I've just described, but watching your words will go a long way to helping you be a better leader. Your words can either instigate conflict—hurting and damaging relationships with your family members—or promote healing, cooperation and better relationships.

Just as with most things in life, there is a flip side to watching your words. You can also program yourself in terms of how you respond to words spoken to you. If you worry about what everyone thinks or says, or if you accept what they say as fact, it can have a negative effect on you. My philosophy is that if someone I don't know or don't respect says something about me that isn't true, I forgive them and move on. At least, that is how it works in theory. If the criticism *is* true, I forgive myself and make an effort to change my behavior. If the statement is made by someone I do respect and love, but I don't agree with it, I talk to the person about his or her feelings regarding my behavior.

My dad, whom I love and respect, once told me I was being selfish with my time. His mother, my grandmother, was in a nursing home and I had not been by to see her in several weeks.

I was in college and had a lot going on. His words hurt me, and I was sure he was wrong. I thought about all the unselfish things I did, and his criticism just didn't make sense. So I told my dad that I was hurt by what he said—and then he explained why he thought my behavior was selfish: I allowed for a certain amount of time for others and when that allotment was up, well, there was no more. I justified my absence at the nursing home because of the areas of my life in which I was unselfish. But it doesn't work that way. Five unselfish acts do not cancel out one selfish act. That behavior is still selfish. I told my dad I appreciated him calling me out on this. When my grandmother passed away, I was never sorry for the time I had spent with her.

Proverbs 18:21 says, "The tongue has the power of life and death" (*NIV*). Remember that your words are powerful. They can be harmful or healing, but either way, they will affect those you love most.

GamePlan

- Be aware of the power of your words. Can you recall any harmful statements you have made to your wife, kids or friends? Apologize to them for the hurtful things you have said. Commit to watching your words more closely.

- Be careful not to speak seemingly harmless statements over yourself or your family that are actually derogatory or destructive. For instance, maybe you've said:

  - You're killing me.
  - You're acting like a girl.
  - You sissy.
  - You are a pig.
  - You are a baby.
  - You are dressed like a prostitute.

Commit to weeding these types of casual curses out of your conversation.

- Get in the habit of giving constructive instruction versus criticism. Start by asking your spouse or your kids questions about their behavior or actions instead of slamming them. Then affirm the good that you see in them and offer suggestions for handling a situation differently in the future. Make healthy communication the norm in your house both by modeling it yourself and by requiring it from your family members as they interact with one another.

- Speak blessings over your wife and kids every day. I speak a blessing over my boys in the morning by saying, "I bless you in the name of the Lord Jesus Christ. You are a child of God with a divine purpose. You have the power of the living God inside of you."

13

Give Respect to Get It

I can't think of any man in the NFL for whom I have more respect than Tony Dungy. Coach Dungy is a Christian man who doesn't just profess his faith but also embodies it. He has great communication skills, is known as a motivator and, unlike a lot of NFL coaches, also has a reputation for being levelheaded and calm. He is a great leader. Whenever I am around Coach Dungy, I just feel peaceful.

The first time I really had time to talk in depth with him was at the AFCA Convention in Orlando, Florida. Coach Dungy was there to accept the Tuss McLaughry Award. I have had many clients who played for Coach Dungy, and we have a number of mutual friends, but I'd never before been in an environment where we could actually talk. I went up to say hello and reintroduce myself.

After I had greeted him and told him my name, he said, "So, you are Drew Pittman."

I'm thinking, *This guy is good. He's making me feel special and acting like he knows who I am.* He went on to tell me that when Tim Tebow was coming out of college, Mr. Tebow called him and asked if he knew any Christian agents. Coach Dungy said he didn't, but that he would call some GMs and ask if they knew of any. He said he called a handful and he kept hearing my name. Of course, this made me feel great, but the point of what I'm telling you here is about *him*, not me. He could have just been pleasant and kind without telling me that story. Coach Dungy gives respect and in turn that respect comes back to him.

To a man, my NFL clients who have played for Coach Dungy have had nothing but good things to say about him. He never raised his voice or felt the need to belittle players for their mistakes. He demanded excellence from his team but didn't feel it was necessary to scream or use profanity to get his point across. Coach Dungy earned the respect of others because he consistently gave it: to his players, to his staff, and to the club's owner.

If you ever hear Coach Dungy speak, you will find out quickly that he is a man from a hard-working family. His mother and father were strong influences in his life, and they taught him to be the man he is today. You will also find out that football was and is a big part of his life. He played quarterback at the University of Minnesota, and after being undrafted in 1976, he signed a free agent contract with the Pittsburgh Steelers. There, he was moved to defensive back. Dungy developed a great deal of respect for his head coach at the Steelers, Chuck Knoll. Knoll was known as one of the great NFL coaches of his era. As a player, Dungy earned the respect of Coach Knoll by being a great competitor and a strong but quiet leader.

In his own coaching career, after stints as a defensive backs coach and a couple of defensive coordinator positions, Coach Dungy was hired as the head football coach to bring the Tampa Bay Buccaneers back from the abyss of the NFL cellar. Coach Dungy had four winning seasons out of six at the helm of the Bucs. He went to the playoffs four times. In 2002 he took the helm of the Indianapolis Colts, a team that had gone 6-10 the previous year; under Dungy, they went 10-6. Coach Dungy won five divisional championships and one Super Bowl. He never had a losing season in seven seasons as the head coach of the Colts. He is the winningest coach in franchise history. Coach Dungy is respected on the football field and off of it—and he got there by giving respect first.

What is the respect factor in your home? I'll admit there are times when I feel like nothing I say carries any weight. One of the most difficult challenges in my home is getting my kids to show respect. A recent revelation in this area of frustration opened my eyes to the truth I'm sharing with you now: In my request for, or requirement of, respect, I needed to model it by *giving* respect. This goes for every relationship, but it is magnified in the home.

You may already know this, especially if you're in or have been through the adolescent years with your children, but teenagers think they know everything. Also, they are pretty sure you don't know anything. My teenager is a great boy overall, and sometimes I have to laugh, because his rough edges remind me of me at his age. One time he gave me a look when I told him something about driving our Ranger. You may know this look. It's the one that says, *You are the dumbest person on the planet.* It didn't matter to him that he was only 14 and didn't even have his driver's license. I was about to give him the "I'm the Dad" treatment when I busted out laughing instead. He knew what he had done, and he was surprised by my reaction. So was I for that matter. By way of an explanation, I told him a story about something that had happened to me when I was 16.

I had just gotten my driver's license and was leaving to go over to a friend's house. As I was on my way out, my mom informed me that at dusk it can be hard to see certain things—like kids running in the street, or animals on the curb—that you would normally be able to see just fine. She was trying to help, but I gave her the same look Jake had just given me. He laughed so hard as he realized I was not going to try to prove that I was the smartest one in the house. I showed some weakness and it was a way of showing him respect. I also told him that I had found out later that the whole light at dusk thing—the thing I thought my mom was stupid for sharing—was real.

Whenever we make big decisions at our house, I make sure to include everyone. We were trying to decide where to go for our summer vacation one time, and I included my then seven-year-old. During the discussion, he made a point that the rest of us had overlooked. You might be surprised by the level of competence your young ones show when given the opportunity to be involved in some of the family's planning and decision-making. Even if their ideas are not always the greatest, when you show them respect by giving them the opportunity to be involved, you will find that they give you more respect. Instead of building a wall, you can build a bridge. The process also gives you a chance to teach your kids the hows and whys of making sound decisions.

I have noticed quarterbacks, general managers, head coaches, company presidents and even politicians who have figured this out. They let the people in their care know that they have a voice—that their opinions matter and are being considered. Teams tend to follow leaders who do this. If you feel you are not getting respect in your home, check to see that you are being respectful. This holds true for your spouse as well as your children. I seek my wife's input and I value it. If you do not allow your wife to make decisions—if you do not give her the role she is meant to have—you will increase the tension in your marriage and decrease the respect.

One thing to be careful about here is the difference between fear and respect. In the Bible, fear and respect are synonymous. Not so in the home. My boys will do what I say when I'm towering over them and threatening punishment if they don't obey. That is not respect. That is fear. Don't get me wrong: a little fear is healthy. Your kids need to know that Dad can bring the hammer. They also need to know that if Dad brings the hammer it was deserved. If I am going to get respect, I have to earn it first of all by being worthy of it. When I blow up and yell at my boys for not obeying me, it becomes more difficult for them to respect me. One of the ways we give respect in our household is to have well-defined rules and well-defined consequences for breaking those rules. No screaming. No yelling. Just the administration of justice, as defined by the rules and consequences.

Coach Dungy was respected by his players because he showed them respect. He treated them like men, and he made sure they knew the consequences for not following his rules. If the rules were broken, the perpetrator had to live with the consequences. Coach Dungy didn't indulge in yelling and cussing and going into tirades in front of the team. I have gone off on one of my sons before for not doing what I told him to do. Afterwards I felt terrible. I didn't cuss at him, but I lost my temper. That does not command respect. I feel the Lord has shown me that those fits are a result of my pride. My pride gets damaged when my kids do not obey. This doesn't excuse my kids from disobedience, but it doesn't give them a reason to respect me either.

I try to learn from the mistakes of others as well as my own. Sometimes the best lessons we can learn come from the mistakes that are out there for everyone to see. I like to take note of how others handle their mistakes. I am good friends with a lot of coaches in both the college ranks and the NFL. I am also close with GMs, directors of player personnel, and cap and contract guys. Just about everything they do is visible to the public. They draft players, institute discipline, cut players, make comments on players' performances, negotiate contracts, and sometimes refuse to step up in contract negotiations and let players sign with other teams. I watch how they handle situations with their players or with the media. I have noticed that the truly great leaders are always accountable—when they make a mistake, they take responsibility for it. You can learn a lot about people by watching how they handle mistakes.

If you want to be respected, you don't have to try to do enough cool or important things to give people a reason to respect you. The best things you can do are to give respect to others and to behave in a manner that is worthy of respect.

GamePlan

- Give respect! Be respectful of others, even if the ideas they have are not good ones. Listen and be courteous of their desires. Does your family have a decision to make? Consider input from each family member.

- Teach your family the importance of giving respect to their elders and to people in positions of leadership, even those with whom you don't necessarily agree. Are there authority figures in your children's lives whom they are having difficulty respecting? Discuss steps they can take to show more respect—and then encourage them in their efforts.

- Go over the top in showing respect for your wife in front of your kids. Affirm her abilities, ask for her opinions, and think of other ways to demonstrate that she is your partner. Give your parents respect in front of your kids and when talking about them. Show them; don't just tell them.

14

Embrace Failure

Quarterback Kurt Warner was successful, in part, because he read opposing defenses masterfully. He also knew how to persevere. Warner's story is well documented. He was undrafted out of college, signed as a free agent and was cut by the NFL, stocked groceries in Iowa, played arena football, was re-signed by the NFL and assigned to play in the World League, won NFL and Super Bowl MVP honors, was released by two other NFL teams, and then went back to the Super Bowl with another team.

Just like Warner, one of my clients, Reggie Swinton, learned how vital perseverance could be. Prior to finally making it in Dallas, Reggie had to learn how to come back from adversity and disappointment. Reggie grew up in Little Rock, Arkansas, and like most young men from Little Rock, Reggie dreamed of playing for the University of Arkansas Razorbacks. As a kid, he watched the games on TV, and he even attended a game or two when the Razorbacks played in Little Rock, as they do a couple of times each season. Reggie would watch the players run out of the tunnel and onto the field while thousands of fans "called the hogs." (If you haven't experienced this, you should, at least once.) But things didn't work out for Reggie to play in the hills of Fayetteville, so he went to Murray State, where Arkansas native Houston Nutt was the head football coach.

Even though he was an all-conference receiver and kick return specialist, Reggie went undrafted in the 1998 NFL Draft. He signed a free-agent contract with the Jacksonville Jaguars but was released prior to the start of the season. Reggie landed in the CFL with the Winnipeg Blue Bombers in 1999 and enjoyed moderate success, only to be released after the season. In 2000, Reggie played for the Arkansas Twisters in the Arena League but was released midway through the season. After a failed attempt to make the Seattle Seahawks, Reggie signed with the WWF league of football, the XFL, where he was once again told he wasn't good enough and was released. He then re-signed with the Twisters in Arkansas. I took Reggie on as a client in the summer of 2001, and in August of that year he signed a contract with the Dallas Cowboys. Needless to say, he had walked a long road, and persistence was the only thing keeping Reggie headed toward his dream.

Reggie enjoyed a successful five-year stint with the Cowboys as a wide receiver and as an outstanding kick return specialist. He could make split-second decisions about where the lane was most likely to open up on a return. In 2002, Reggie was one of only two players to return both a punt and a kickoff for touchdowns. Reggie went on to play for the Green Bay Packers, the Detroit Lions, the Houston Texans and the Arizona Cardinals (where, coincidentally, he was a teammate of Warner's) before he retired. Reggie used to say with some sense of pride that he was cut from every professional football league around. The pride in that statement came from the resiliency required to live through that type of rejection. It is a tribute to his determination.

There are many parents who "joystick" their children through life, completing their homework, making excuses for them with their coaches as to why they didn't perform well in the game, and making decisions for them in every area of life. I used to stand on the sidelines as a soccer coach, yelling instructions to the boys on what to do and when to do it. The players didn't have to think; I was thinking for them—just joysticking them around the field. I eventually learned that that style of coaching actually hinders players, as they don't ever learn how to make decisions for themselves. I was embarrassed when I realized what I was doing on the soccer field. I was more embarrassed when I realized I was doing the same thing with my kids in life. I would make sure they had their lunches and their homework before leaving for school instead of teaching them to think of these things for themselves.

The consequences of making bad decisions or of not thinking are usually the best teachers.

You may be one of these parents. If you are, don't feel bad. The motivation is always love for your kids. However, the result could be that you are contributing to a generation of adults who can't make decisions for themselves and aren't equipped to handle failure. In order to create a winning family, a leader builds one that embraces, learns from and even celebrates failure. I am not saying that when your son or daughter chooses not to study for a test and brings home a failing grade, you should throw a party. I am saying that you may not need to scream at your child and ground him or her. Failure is an opportunity to coach your kids through their decision-making processes and give them better options for the next time. Don't forget the consequences, but make sure they're fitting for the behavior.

Another part of the coaching process is to teach your kids not to be afraid of making decisions and not to be afraid of failing. When my youngest son, Eli, was just beginning to learn how to ride a bike, he was pretty shaky. But he took off up the driveway one afternoon, swerving from side to side. He was scared to venture out but he did it anyway. We live out in the country, and the driveway was surrounded by fairly rough land. About halfway up the driveway, he veered too far to his left and couldn't recover. He ended up falling over into a cactus. It was not a pretty sight, and I spent a good amount of time pulling tiny cactus quills out of his sweet little hand and wiping tears off his cheeks. He was a tough little guy, though, and as Layne and I coached him on how his decision could be better next time, instead of being afraid to ride that bike again, he decided to make sure he started on the main road, far from the perils of wild cacti.

Some of the greatest benefits of playing sports are the life lessons you learn. Sports teach you that you can push yourself beyond what you thought was possible. Sports teach you how to be a humble victor. Sports teach you how to handle defeat with grace. Sports teach you teamwork, character, determination and perseverance and help you develop a strong work ethic. But sports should also teach creativity and good decision-making skills. I have seen many NFL players who can make excellent decisions in a split second because of the situations they have been in on the field. In some of these situations, they have failed. Linemen learn how to adjust their blocking schemes on the fly as the defense shifts pre-snap when they've first failed to do so. Return men like Swinton learn how to make the right cut by first making the wrong cut. Linebackers learn how to take better angles to the running back after taking a bad angle and giving up a touchdown. Players learn how to make these lightning-fast decisions by being allowed to make them—and they all make a bunch of wrong decisions before they get it right.

We have some friends whose goal in life is to make sure their kids get straight As in school. That doesn't sound like a terrible thing on the surface. What these parents are willing to do to ensure their kids get an A is where the issues arise. There was a project for the seventh grade where the kids were told to build a replica of a national monument. When I was in school that kind of assignment meant we got to eat a lot of popsicles so we could use the sticks to build the Washington Monument or the Empire State Building. One of our adult friends took a different tack as she helped her son with his project. She spent over $100 on supplies and stayed up all night, three nights in a row, to get it finished. When my wife questioned this friend about keeping her son up all night, and how on earth he could make it through the day, she confessed that Johnny didn't stay up. She did! Then she proceeded to justify her behavior by explaining how unfair it was to give a seventh-grader a task like this and saying that if she hadn't done it her son wouldn't have received a good grade. *Are you kidding me?!* I could not believe what I was hearing.

You may be saying, "So what? I would have done the same thing." Are you so intent on your kids succeeding that you forget they need to learn how to fail? Of course you don't want them to become good at failing, or even used to it, but at some point they will fail—and if they aren't ready for it, they won't know how to handle it. My personal opinion is that failure can be a great motivator. What is that little thing that makes you give the extra effort it sometimes takes to succeed? For me, at least on occasion, it is knowing how bad failing feels. Our kids need to feel it so they know they don't want to feel it again. They need to feel it so they will do what it takes not to fail in worse ways in the future. We will not always be there to make decisions for them.

If our children don't learn how to fail—and how to avoid failure by doing what it takes to succeed—as young people, it will become an issue for them at some point later on. It seems like most people in our society are in one of two camps: There are those who don't give a rip about what their kids do, and there are others so consumed with their children's success that they will go to any lengths to ensure their kids' succeed. Neither end of this spectrum is healthy; we need to find that place in the middle where we give our children room to fail so that they learn how to pursue success for themselves

The success experienced by Warner and Swinton teaches us a valuable lesson: Your life will be shaped by failure—not by avoiding it, but by how you respond to it. Reggie used to tell me that every time he was released, he took time to look within himself and determine what he could do better, how he could work harder, and what part of his game he needed to improve in order for this never to happen to him again. If you can teach your kids how to learn from failure and even to embrace it, they will be much better equipped to handle it.

GamePlan

- Assess your own attitude toward failure. Are you afraid of failure? If so, find a friend or mentor who can help you work through your fear.

- How can you help your wife be more confident about making choices and taking risks—even if it means sometimes she will fail?

- Do you allow your children to make age-appropriate decisions? How can you support them the next time they have a decision to make? You may want to offer your input, but let the decision be theirs; don't make it for them.

- There can be multiple correct answers to many problems or circumstances. Encourage creativity as your family members think through the issues and choices they face.

- Let your family know it's okay to make mistakes! We learn more from our mistakes than anything else. As leaders, we need to learn from our own mistakes, but also to use mistakes as teachable moments for others. If your family is too afraid to make mistakes, they will be paralyzed.

15

Huddle Up

When you consider the heroes of a football game, you probably don't think immediately of the offensive linemen. They are the guys in the trenches who do the dirty work. One of my offensive line clients, Nate Garner of the Miami Dolphins, is valued by his teammates, but like most offensive linemen, he is relatively unknown by most NFL fans. I was watching the Dolphins play the Carolina Panthers a few years ago, and I witnessed one of the most amazing feats I have seen in a football game. No, it wasn't an acrobatic catch or a long, zig-zagging run. It was an amazing display of football intelligence made possible by a communication system that had been perfected over time.

Garner was the sixth man on the Dolphins' offensive line, but unlike most sixth men, Garner is capable of playing any position on the line. Most offensive linemen are a center, a guard or a tackle. Most linemen are more comfortable either on the right side or on the left side. Switching sides means changing your footwork, and that is not something usually done overnight. A change to the other side of the center generally takes a whole training camp to master and, once it's done, it's done—you don't flip sides. Some linemen can, as they say in the business, swing inside or outside. Swinging outside means a center could play some guard, or a guard could play some tackle—if they had to. Swinging inside is when a tackle could fill in at guard if the situation required it, or a guard could fill in at center. But Garner is adept at every position on both sides of the line, something that is highly unusual in the NFL.

On this particular occasion, Garner had started the game at right guard but had injured his ankle when a defensive tackle rolled up on him after he pulled on a trap play. Garner came out to get his ankle taped. The trainers were just finishing up when an assistant coach started yelling for Garner. Another lineman had gone down and Garner was needed to go back in. The Dolphins were driving and had the momentum. Garner jumped off the training table and heard the play from the assistant coach as he ran onto the field. The team had broken the huddle, and Garner's teammate who was playing center slid over to guard. It had been roughly eight seconds since Garner had jumped off the training table on the sidelines and headed for the field, with fans screaming and his own adrenalin pumping—thinking he was going in at guard.

Now Garner was approaching the line of scrimmage as the center, and in a split second he had to remap his brain to run the play with a whole new set of responsibilities. As if that wasn't enough, the QB told him he had changed the play in the huddle. The communication between the QB and Garner had to be quick and concise. They spoke a language they had rehearsed many times in practice for such a time as this. Once again, Garner had to download the play, comprehend his responsibilities, look at the defensive front, call the protection, and communicate any changes based on what the defense was showing—all in a matter of seconds under the bright lights of a packed NFL stadium. Because the QB could communicate to Garner and Garner could communicate to his fellow offensive linemen, the play was successful. The Dolphins kept the drive going and eventually scored a touchdown.

Is communication a tripping point in your home? How many times have you watched a fight erupt or listened to a friend talk about a problem in his house that obviously started as a result of poor communication? Think about a quarterback going into a game. He leans into the huddle and says, "Here we go, men, 40-streak, jet right 1, V straight, deep scat, option ringo." If his teammates have never heard this terminology before, they will have no clue what they are supposed to do. There is no chance that the play goes off and a significant chance that the QB gets pulverized. This is what can happen in your home if you are speaking a language your family doesn't understand, or if they are speaking a language you don't understand. If you and your family are using different playbooks, huddle up, get in the same book, and then get on the same page of that book.

My job as a leader is to make sure the lines of communication are open and that the communication is clear. When a player goes to a new team, the first thing he learns is the terminology. I am amazed at how many different ways football teams can describe the same simple assignments. There are many things that may cause miscommunication in your world. It is your job to make sure your expectations are understood, and it is also your job to make sure your family's expectations are understood. This can be especially challenging with kids. They don't know, inherently, how to communicate clearly, so they need to be taught. If you are going to teach them, you must be able to communicate clearly yourself.

The most common mistake in fumbled communication is the making of assumptions. My friend Steve travels a lot for business. His wife told him she felt their oldest son, who was 16 at the time, needed some quality time doing man stuff with his dad. Steve said he'd take his son deer hunting over the Christmas holidays. They took off early the first day of the break. Steve's wife figured they'd be gone a few days. When Steve and his son got home seven days later, Steve was shocked to find his wife angry that he'd spent the whole vacation deer hunting. Steve had actually expected praise when he got home, so he was quite miffed to discover his wife wasn't speaking to him. A little more communication with fewer assumptions would have gone a long way in this situation.

Another key to staying on the same page is making sure our families know that when they have unfavorable news to deliver, we will not react negatively. While we shouldn't lower our expectations, we need to let our families know that we can handle difficult things calmly. A bad report card, being cut from the team, a fender bender or other such situations should be met with calmness and compassion. Our first reaction to bad news can't be disgust or anger. Rather, we can start with something like, "I am so glad you felt comfortable enough to share that with me."

One of my best friends has a 15-year-old daughter (we'll call her "Mandy") who, like her mom and dad, is Type A and independent. She is a great young lady and is outgoing, talented and beautiful.

She's been challenging to parent, but in a good way. Mandy was talking to my friend, her dad, the other day and was noticeably upset at her boyfriend. My friend asked her what was wrong, and Mandy blurted out that her boyfriend was mad at her because she "won't put out." She said that all her friends had lost their virginity in the past year, but that she was not going there. I am sure the conversation would have been different if she had confessed that she had given herself completely to this young man! But whatever the specifics, my friend was deeply thankful that his daughter felt close enough to speak so openly to him—and he took care to respond to what she had shared without flying off the handle. He didn't go get his shotgun or make emotionally charged statements like forbidding her to see her boyfriend ever again. He let Mandy know that it was safe to confide in him about sensitive subjects. I am constantly setting the bar high for my boys but I'm also letting them know I understand that sometimes they will make mistakes or face struggles in doing the right thing. I also make sure they know that when they do, I will not blow up at them. I want them to know I am there to help correct bad behavior lovingly and with grace, and I will be there for them in whatever difficult situations they find themselves, whether through their own questionable choices or the actions of others.

In my home, we literally huddle up. I credit my wife with this idea. We sit down regularly and talk about what is going on in our lives. It is a time for the kids to open up. Anything and everything is on the table. They can talk about how we have treated them or how they have treated each other. It is a time for us to compliment them on certain behaviors or to share where they are falling short of expectations. Because we have established a family culture, we have a clear framework within which we can discuss behaviors that don't meet the expectations of that culture. We call this time Family Circle. I will admit that my boys roll their eyes every time. They never want to participate—at first. But we do it anyway. It is usually productive and will yield even more noticeable benefits as the years go on. You can adjust your Huddle Up time based on the ages of your kids and their maturity levels. Don't be discouraged if the participation isn't great initially. As the old Nike commercial used to say, *Just Do It.*

I encourage you to have a one-on-one huddle with your wife from time to time as well. This is not a time to list the things you wish she would do better, but a time to ask her what she needs more of or less of from you. It's a time to check her pulse on how she is feeling about your marriage and a time to pray together. I hope you are talking and praying together regularly, but this is a time specifically designed to clear the air. If you are like me, you probably save some conversations for "when the time is right." By having a set time and avenue to get things out, you can avoid the inevitable blow up. It usually isn't one thing that flips the switch and triggers a blow up; it is the cumulative effect of many things held in. It's helpful when there's an established right time to air things out before the pressure becomes too great.

One area of communication I can improve on is my inability to say, "I am sorry; I was wrong." It is hard for me to even write the words here! I usually feel when I am "wrong," it is because my wife or my kids didn't hear me well enough or they are being unreasonable or some other equally ridiculous rationalization. I do not like to be wrong. I am not good at it, even though I should be with all the practice I get. It just feels *yucky* to me. God has shown me that this is my problem and it's one rooted in pride. I am learning that saying *I'm sorry* is freeing. By apologizing to my kids or my wife, and asking for their forgiveness, I am modeling the strength that is found in humility.

Whatever your particular challenges in this area, clear communication, and a regular venue to host it, will go a long way to improving your team.

GamePlan

- Speak the same language. Unclear communication or a lack of communication can cause conflict. Huddle up regularly with your family. These family circles are opportunities for each family member to share honestly about how they are feeling and what's going on in their life. Lead the way by communicating openly yourself.

- Be clear about what you are saying and what you are hearing. If what someone says isn't clear, don't make assumptions. A few minutes of clarification on the front end can save a world of hurt later on.

- Learn how to say "I'm sorry; I was wrong," or "I need help." Lead your family in humbly asking for forgiveness or help.

16

Own Your Actions

One of my good friends, former general manager for the Miami Dolphins Jeff Ireland, once told me he would rather sign a player he knew he could depend on to do the right thing than one he had to guess about. Moreover, Ireland claims he can *win* with dependable players who own up to their shortcomings, but he can't win with players who have an excuse—or someone to blame—for every mistake, regardless of their ability.

NFL teams go to great lengths to find out what type of athlete a player is. They spend millions of dollars every year on scouting and analysis to determine who will have the best chance to be successful on their team, in their system, with their coaching staffs. Craig and I have a saying about the NFL scouting system. We call it *NFL Overkill*. Teams will send a scout to a school in August or September. They will go back in October or November. If the grade is high enough, they will send another scout to cross check—or they might send their national scout to "go over the top." They will evaluate these same players at all-star games and work them out at the Scouting Combine in February. After the Combine, these prospects will work out at their own schools; this workout is called Pro Day. And that's where you'll find all the NFL scouts who worked them out at the Combine. Some teams will then put certain players through individual workouts by position coaches— the same coaches who worked the same players out at the Scouting Combine. Thus: *NFL Overkill!*

The one test they have not come up with is how to measure a player's heart or character. There are *signs* but no foolproof test. One NFL GM told me that one reason they spend a large amount of resources on NFL Overkill is so they can actually spend time with the prospects. He told me that the more they're around a player, the better feel they have for what type of person the player is. This GM feels that a player could put on a good front in a 30-minute interview in Indianapolis, or in a 5-minute conversation in the lobby of the Senior Bowl hotel, but that he wouldn't be able to keep it up from August to April. The team scouts will eventually find out what the player is made of, and one of the key character traits almost every team is looking for is accountability.

Players' learning to take responsibility for their behavior is critical to the success of any team. I will admit that this didn't come easy for me. As a child, I loved to be outside playing with my friends. I could usually be found somewhere in the neighborhood playing the sport that was in season or else over at a friend's home. I would always have a specific time when I was supposed to be home. Unfortunately, I was pretty bad about being home at the appointed time. As that hour approached, all the best fun would just begin. I am sure it just *seemed* like that, but I didn't want to miss anything. I remember walking or riding my bike home, all the while working on my excuse for why I was late. There had to be *something* that wasn't my fault. I came up with some great stories, but my parents still made sure I understood that I had to be accountable for my actions. I was responsible for getting home on time and, no matter what happened "outside of my control," I needed to be accountable when I didn't make it. As I got older, and the responsibilities were greater, the requirement for accountability did not change. In fact, the older I got, the greater the need for accountability.

I have seen a lot of football players who have learned this concept and a lot who haven't. Every player has a role on a team, and every player needs to handle his responsibilities on the field for the team to be successful. When I go see my players during an NFL season, I usually arrive on a Saturday and spend some time with them before they report to the team hotel. A couple of hours before the game starts, I generally get on the field while the teams are going through their pre-game routines. This gives me a chance to talk to the team's front office personnel and coaches face-to-face. I like to get their read on my client—how he is progressing and what he can do to get better. I get a feel for how the team perceives his attitude, work ethic, and other factors. After the game, I go to dinner with my client and we talk about the game, the season, and what I have found out from the team. Most of the players I represent are harder on themselves than anybody else is on them. This is one of the qualities I look for when I recruit a player. I want guys who are accountable. Sometimes the mistake on the field started in the meeting room or on the practice field or even during the off-season. The NFL is a business, with strict expectations for its employees, and players have to treat it that way or they won't last long.

I was at a Carolina Panthers game last season, and one of their defensive backs was struggling. He got beat on a deep ball. Instead of shaking it off, as a defensive back should do, he started yelling at the safety. The team was pretty good at disguising their coverages, but it was obvious the guy had his receiver in man-to-man coverage. When the group came off the field, the secondary coach made a beeline for the player who had gotten beat and gave him an earful. Obviously I couldn't hear the conversation, but I didn't need to. I could tell that the player did not own his mistake. He was arguing and yelling. He was pointing at the safety, and he even threw his helmet for effect. Now, no one likes to get their tail chewed out, especially not in front of 70,000 fans and a national television audience, but the professional—the accountable player—usually says, "Yes, sir," and vows to his coach that he will do better next time.

I started teaching this concept to my sons when they were quite young. They didn't know what accountability meant, so I told them it meant to "own their actions." My wife and I strive to model this principle for them too. I know a bunch of excuse makers and they drive me crazy. Sometimes I catch myself being an excuse maker and I have to stop myself. My boys know that it is not just okay to make a mistake—it is inevitable. I want my sons to learn how to make decisions and not be afraid of the outcome—as long as the decisions are thought through and are made with common sense and character. Our kids will be better off if we stop thinking for them, making excuses for them, and even taking the blame for them, and start teaching them how to make their own decisions and own their actions. I heard a new term the other day: *The Hero Parent*. Hero Parents are always there to rescue their children. Your kids will fail and so will mine. If they understand this—and understand that it's okay to fail—they will be well on their way to owning their actions.

Now the hard part: If we are going to ask our kids to own their actions, we must do the same. How are you at owning your actions? How about your wife? Personally, I find it easier to be accountable for things relating to work or with my friends than I do for things at home. I don't like acknowledging that I've made mistakes or done the wrong things around my wife or my kids. Nevertheless, it is vital that we model accountability for our children—and sometimes for our spouses as well.

My friend Paul has two awesome kids and an incredible wife. His son is smart, personable, and just an all-around great kid. *And* the boy has an issue with admitting that he's wrong. Paul gets frustrated with the constant, "I didn't hear you," or "I was going to right after this." Unfortunately, Paul's son might be learning this behavior from his mom, Paul's wife. When it comes to letting her family down in even a small way, she tends to deflect the guilt. Paul finally sat down with her and, in a kind and loving way, shared with her his frustration. She was defensive at first, but Paul was kind and gracious. He admitted that he could improve in this area too. Eventually his wife broke down and revealed that the problem stemmed from an area of insecurity. Her father had always demanded perfection. When she couldn't live up to that standard, she deflected the blame. Her father probably had great intentions, but the lesson here is that requiring perfection sets your child up for failure and can lead to other issues—avoidable ones. After their conversation about accountability, Paul's wife said she felt as though she'd been set free, and that she didn't want the kids to learn a bad habit, especially from her.

When a mistake is made—when feelings are hurt or when bounds are overstepped—family members need to take responsibility for their behavior. Learning and practicing this high level of accountability is a critical step toward building a winning family.

GamePlan

- Be the best model of accountability your kids will ever see. When have you made a mistake that affected your family? How did you handle it? Take ownership of your mistakes.

- Have a conversation about owning your actions at your next huddle. Let family members discuss how they feel when others don't own their actions. Encourage them to be honest about their own mistakes and shortcomings.

- Make sure your family knows that even though it can feel burdensome, being accountable actually sets you free. Share a story from your own experience to illustrate this point.

- Teach accountability rather than quickly responding with correction and discipline. Remind your kids to make good, thoughtful choices, but that if they fail, they can talk to you and find positive ways to move forward.

17

Let Your Faith Be Infectious

A few years ago, I signed Daniel Sepulveda as a client after being told I was not in the running. I was talking to Daniel's dad, Carlos, who was overseeing the agent selection process. Carlos is a successful businessman and a wonderful human being. As the CEO of Interstate Batteries, Carlos led the company to the top of the industry. I knew Daniel was the type of person I wanted to work with, not only because he was supremely talented, but also because he had an infectious personality.

At the time, I was not aware of how mature he was in his faith. I just knew there was something about him that made me sure he was my kind of guy. So I fought for him. After asking a series of questions and suggesting a creative way to structure our relationship, I got back in the game and eventually I signed Daniel to a representation agreement. I then quickly found out what it was that had drawn me to Daniel. He has a confidence in who he is—and *whose* he is—that makes girls giddy and guys want to hang out with him. (Okay, his athletic build and rugged good looks also have a little to do with the girls being giddy.)

Daniel is one of only two players to win the prestigious Ray Guy Award, which is presented each year to the best punter in college football, twice. Daniel has experienced a roller coaster of highs and lows in his career—both during college and in the pros. He followed his older brother to Baylor as a walk-on linebacker.

He redshirted his freshman year. The following season started with an unforeseen event that would alter the course of Daniel's career and life.

The Baylor special teams coach was asking for volunteers to try out for the role of punter. Despite not having punted since his junior year in high school, Daniel decided to give it a shot. He just wanted to be on the field. He won the job and was awarded a scholarship. In only his second year as a punter, he won his first Ray Guy Award and was a consensus All-American. He tore his ACL his junior year and sat out the whole season. Determined, he returned his senior year and won the Ray Guy Award again— and this time was a unanimous All-American. Daniel's strong senior season was parlayed into being a fourth-round pick of the Pittsburgh Steelers. After a solid rookie year, his second season was cut short by another ACL injury. I was on my way from the Detroit Lions training camp to Latroub, Pennsylvania, where the Steelers have conducted their training camp for many years.

I received a call while changing planes in Atlanta. It was Daniel and he said, "I have some bad news." Those are words you never want to hear, but for a sports agent during training camp they are especially ominous. When he told me about the injury, I assured him I'd be there in a few hours. Upon arriving at camp, I was escorted to the training facility, where Daniel and the team orthopedic doctor were waiting on me. We looked at the MRI and the doctor explained the options.

I finally asked the question: "When are you going to learn that your job is to punt, and the other 10 guys are supposed to make the tackle?" When a punter gets hurt, it is usually because his punt coverage broke down and he tried to save the day with a touchdown-saving tackle. When you are as big, strong and athletic as Daniel is, you want to prove to your teammates that you are not just a punter. You are a football player.

Daniel looked at me sheepishly and told me he was jogging a little out route with the other specialists before practice. When he made a slow and seemingly harmless cut, the knee just popped. And now there we were in the training room discussing surgical options. Daniel was forced to sit and watch the whole season, including the Steelers' Super Bowl victory. Daniel performed well in his third season, but the Steelers didn't make it to the big game that year.

The fourth season of Daniel's up-and-down career brought yet another challenge. While (you guessed it) making a tackle following a booming punt, he tore his MCL. To make matters worse, the Steelers went to the Super Bowl *again* and Daniel was forced to watch, *again*, the one game every player dreams of. The beleaguered punter could easily have grown bitter, but he remained joyful. Why? He says he knows God has a plan for him that is bigger and better than his plan—and even bigger and better than football. Daniel's faith sustains him, and his coaches and teammates have taken notice of this over the years.

During Daniel's first Super Bowl experience, he was interviewed on media day about the unavoidable disappointment of not being able to play. The media was baiting him, trying to get him to voice his frustration and disappointment. They prodded him to lash out about how unfair it was to miss the Super Bowl. Daniel explained that while he would love to be preparing to actually play in the game, he had learned a great deal about himself and his faith during the year. He could not explain his lack of bitterness any way other than the peace of God. Daniel would share with the growing throng of reporters how he missed the practices, the camaraderie and the emotion of the games. He also offered an account of the opportunities he'd had over the course of the season to share his faith in the greater Pittsburgh area. He was no stranger to sharing the words, but what made that year special was that he was able to *show* his faith too. It wasn't just words this time; he got to live it.

It's one thing to talk about loving Jesus or trusting God; it's another thing to *do* it. That's what we're all made for. Forget the worldly culture that says you should keep your faith to yourself—that it's a personal thing. It *is* personal, but nowhere in the Bible does it tell you to keep it to yourself. What's more, wearing a W.W.J.D. bracelet and putting a fish symbol on your car are not the end game. I am trying to be better about living my faith—letting it be evident by the choices I make, the words I speak, and my overall attitude. If I say the joy of the Lord is my strength, but I can't handle a little setback, what message am I sending? If you say your peace comes from your trust in Jesus, but you're always stressed about money or your kids, are you drawing people to seek what you have?

If you haven't figured it out by now, I believe your leadership starts in your home. It's the same for me! If I am doing a good job "out in the world" but am not having a positive effect in my own home, I am missing the mark. My kids need to see me walk out my faith. I have found it is easier to talk about my faith than to put it into practice, especially at home.

When my wife was diagnosed with rheumatoid arthritis in 2003, it rocked our world. She went from running marathons and looking like she could kick my butt to becoming a frail shadow of her former self. It even hurt her to breathe! It was a scary and difficult time. Our boys were young and they didn't understand what was happening, but they could sense that something was going on. Layne and I both grew (and continue to grow) in our faith through dealing with this trial. As we did so, of course, our sons were watching. I want my kids to want the faith I have. I want my faith to be one *worth* wanting. I wear a cross necklace, a James Avery cross ring, and a cool "Jesus fish" bracelet. But if I don't show my faith in my actions, I'm just wearing jewelry. I once heard a guy say, about being polite, "If you have to tell people you are, you probably aren't." It's the same with faith. If you have to tell people you have it, you probably don't. I want mine to be obvious.

I don't know why Daniel had to deal with so many physical struggles during his NFL career. After his second disappointing missed-Super Bowl season, the Steelers decided not to re-sign him, fearing he was not going to be able to play again. Daniel took a year off to allow his leg to completely heal. After the year off, he had an opportunity to join the Arizona Cardinals, but once again his knee reminded him that football was in the past, and he retired. I believe that if he hadn't had these injuries, he could have played a long time and been known as one of the best punters the game had ever seen. I also believe that Daniel could have justified being bitter and angry. He had a good enough reason to lash out at God. The fact that he didn't shows the strength of his faith.

Circumstances will change over the course of your life, but true faith creates a lasting and immovable foundation. You need to own your faith and pass it on to your children as well. God sustained me, and rose up in me, during the most difficult period of Layne's illness. And it was during that tough season that I was blessed to pray the prayer of faith with both of my sons, and even had the privilege of baptizing them. There is no greater key to a winning family than a genuine, infectious faith.

GamePlan

- An infectious faith is a developed faith. It's important to develop the disciplines of faith: daily Bible reading, consistent prayer life, serving in a church family, giving of your resources, being in fellowship as a family with other believers, being discipled, discipling someone else, and pursuing fellowship with other God-seeking men. Take stock of your own faith life. What areas are doing well and what areas need work? Commit to strengthening your faith life.

- Welcome opportunities to walk out your faith. What trials or challenges are you facing? Ask the Lord what He wants you to learn and how you can grow in your faith. Avoid the temptation to dwell on the question, *Why is this happening to me?*

- Talk out your faith with your family. Your children will benefit from hearing you discuss how your relationship with God affects how you face the challenges and choices in your life.

- In your next family huddle, talk about areas in which family members could better live out their faith. Grow together in your faith walk, and watch how others respond to your family's infectious faith.

18

Play to Your Strengths

Long before I dreamed of becoming an NFL agent, I was a soccer player at Southern Methodist University in Texas. During my time as a Mustang, I was asked to play defender, even though I was better suited to play forward (the position I had always played). When forced to play outside of my strengths, I did not play with excellence—and my love for the game waned. It wasn't that I didn't want to play wherever I was needed to help my team win; I just wasn't a good defender. We played our closest rival, the University of North Texas, and they had a forward from Denmark who was outstanding. Our coach, Jim Benedict, decided to have me mark him, which is soccer lingo for *cover him* or *guard him*. Wherever my mark went, I should be there. Coach Benedict even proposed that if the Danish forward went off the field and sat on the bench, he wanted to see me sitting next to him. That was all fine and good except for one detail: I was not very good at marking players. I was not playing to my strengths, and while things worked out alright in that game, I didn't enjoy it—and that was the beginning of the end to my soccer career.

Similar situations often arise in other sports. I once represented a talented running back, Jarrod Baxter, from the University of New Mexico. Jarrod was drafted by the Houston Texans in their inaugural draft. He was moved to fullback shortly after being drafted, and he willingly accepted the move. But the position was outside of his strengths. As a fullback, Jarrod was required to do a lot of blocking, and he didn't carry the ball nearly as often as he was used to from his time playing at New Mexico. Even though

Jarrod was built like a fullback, he had better running instincts than blocking skills. Jarrod had a nice five-year career, especially considering he played a position he was not completely suited for, but I can't help imagining how different things might have been for him had he been able to continue in the role he was great at and loved.

As with Jarrod, your children have been given certain gifts and strengths by God. If you can help them discover their strengths, and then invest energy in helping them cultivate those strengths, you will see them flourish. I remember vividly the day Jake, our first child, was born. As I held him for the first time, Psalm 139:13-16 became so real to me. David speaks of how God knit him together in his mother's womb, and he affirms that he was fearfully and wonderfully made. I could see how God had made my son just exactly as He wanted to, with gifts and talents and desires and passions. The epiphany was expanded when my second son was born. He was *so* different from his older brother. If you have more than one child, I am probably describing your story as well! As parents, we recognize the particular intricacies of our kids—the special quirks and one-of-a-kind personalities. Both of my boys are special. I see many of their mother's traits and my traits in each of them. I also recognize *original* qualities in both of them—awesome things that I have no explanation for, other than that God knew they would need those traits to fulfill their purposes in life.

Eli, my youngest, goes through stages of being totally sold out to certain things. At first it was Thomas the Tank Engine trains. Then it was Legos. He would play for hours with the box sets containing thick instruction booklets. He'd follow the instructions to the letter and build each creation exactly as it was supposed to be built. Then he would tear them apart, mix the sets, and build his own creations. After Legos, Eli got into basketball and was all about looking like a basketball player and playing like his favorite Spurs players or Baylor players. Eli loves his friends, but he also loves to be alone and is comfortable in his own skin.

Jake, on the other hand, is all about the social events. He always wants to be with friends and is loved by all. He loves football and basketball and is accomplished at both. He is also an incredible fisherman. He knows what bait to throw where. He knows when to be out in the middle of the lake and when to hug the coastline. I was flipping through the sports channels the other day and landed on the NCAA Bass Fishing Championship. That is not a misprint. I must admit, my first thought was, *Do they give scholarships for fishing? That would be sweet!*

Both of my boys have demonstrated a great aptitude for soccer. It seemed to come naturally to them, but maybe that was because I started them off kicking the ball around from an early age. As a former soccer player, I was excited about the possibility of them following in my footsteps. As they've gotten older, their love of the game is dwindling. I have to be okay with that—and I am because I know this is their life; I have my own.

Allowing my boys the freedom to be who they are was modeled for me by my own father, who had played college basketball. I was a pretty decent basketball player in junior high, but when I got to high school, my love of soccer took over. I was just better at it. This was probably difficult for my dad. He didn't know the first thing about soccer. Thankfully, he didn't try to live through me and push me to pursue *his* passion. He let me follow my own.

Too often parents push their children to love what they love. It could be their favorite sport, their love of music, or their appreciation of art. The key to each is that it is *theirs*, not their children's. This *pushing* can be seen on youth athletic fields all over our nation. It is usually the dad pushing the child to try harder and be better: win, win, win! Kids play youth sports because it's fun. And it is fun, right up until a parent—often the father—takes the fun out of it. As a youth sports coach, I caution parents against overemphasizing the wrong things. It's the same with other areas of children's lives. If I can teach my boys about the benefits of working hard for what they want, controlling their effort and their behavior, and seeking after the things they are passionate about, then they will be well equipped to make the most of the gifts and strengths they have been given.

I have a good friend who has several kids. One of his sons is a great athlete—a real rugged boy who likes contact sports and "mixing it up." My friend has another son who is always wearing a costume and acting out the part of the character he is dressed as. This child is imaginative and dedicated to his character. It is hard to get him to break character. So while his brother is practicing football or soccer, this boy is playing Spider Man in full costume or Indiana Jones or *Star Wars*. His dad, my friend, is a former Army Ranger and a Purple Heart recipient. In short, he's the definition of a man's man. I am thrilled to see him throw the ball with one son and play the part of an Ewok with the other. He is developing both of his sons' special interests.

Sometimes it is hard for me to let go of the things that have been important to me, but I know I need to let my sons decide what they want to pursue. I have had the opportunity to live my life and they get to live theirs. Maybe you were pushed into something as a child, and so that has become your model now that you're parenting. Please, consider a different approach. Let your children grow and dream and be fired up about whatever God has given them a passion for. Their passion may be different from yours, but that's okay. My friend Ken Coleman says, "Your sweet spot is found at the intersection of your greatest strength and your greatest passion." That is a good place to find—for yourself and for your children.

GamePlan

- Where is your sweet spot? Do your strengths and passions intersect? What changes can you make so that you can play to your strengths and pursue the things God has gifted you for? Discuss with your wife ways you can do this that are good for the whole family.

- How can you support your wife in developing and exercising her gifts and interests? Do what you can to free her up to do the things she loves.

- Help your children find their sweet spots. Encourage them to pursue their interests, even if it means taking risks and stretching themselves.

- Don't live vicariously through your kids. Do your kids' activities reflect their interests, or yours? What expectations for your kids' lives do you need to let go of? How can you help your kids be the unique people God has created them to be?

19

Learn the Art of Motivation

In between my living room and kitchen stands a statue of my father-in-law, Grant Teaff. It is a replica of the one outside of Baylor University's stadium. The pedestal is inscribed with two words: The Believer. That name was given to the statue because Coach Teaff was famous for making his teams believe they could win. His first book was even titled *I Believe*.

One of the most interesting and oft-told stories of Coach Teaff motivating his team is one about him eating a worm. In 1978, the Baylor Bears were preparing to play a stronger University of Texas team. In an attempt to motivate his team right before kick-off, Coach Teaff told a story about a couple of Eskimos who were out fishing. One of them was having great success, but the other one hadn't caught a thing. The Eskimo who was struggling asked his friend how he was doing so well. The successful fisherman responded, "Your worms are frozen." He went on to tell his friend, "You have to keep your worms warm." And at that, the Eskimo opened his mouth and revealed his worms.

Coach Teaff told his team that in order to have great success, one must do the hard things—even the distasteful things. He congratulated his team for a great week of practice. He assured them that they were ready to play. He told them that at this point it was up to them to play the game—and then he added, "But the coaches will keep the worms warm." He opened his mouth and pulled out a worm to show the team. He put it back in his mouth and the team went totally nuts. The Bears beat the Longhorns 38-14 that day.

But the Coach Teaff story I like most is about the team dog he had at McMurry University. There was a stray dog that used to hang out around the practice field, and the team sort of adopted it. It looked like the dog from the *Little Rascals* TV show from back in the day—a big dog full of attitude. The team gave him the name "Ringer" because of the ring around his eye. Coach Teaff would tell the team that Ringer was a lot like them. He would lie by the practice field while the team went through their preparations for that week's opponent, and he was on the sideline during the games.

On a cold Saturday night in the West Texas town of Abilene, McMurry was hosting nationally prominent Arlington State, led by legendary head coach Chena Gilstrap. The two teams had been out on the field going through their pre-game warm-ups, and already words had been exchanged about who was going to come out on top. When the warm-up time was over, the teams went to their respective locker rooms for some last-minute instructions. Coach Teaff had one of his assistants go in to talk about the game plan and also to tell the team that Coach Teaff had something important to share with them.

Coach Teaff stayed outside the locker room for effect. He had been walking from the field to address his team, not feeling particularly fired up about his final comments, when, like a gift from heaven, Ringer came limping around the corner. It was obvious the dog had bitten off a little more than he could chew and had gotten the worst of a dogfight. His ear was bleeding and a big patch of fur on his back was missing. Coach Teaff scooped the big dog up in both arms and kicked open the door to the locker room. When the big metal door hit the concrete wall, the noise startled the players, coaches and football staff. Coach Teaff laid Ringer on the table in the midst of the team and, mustering a tear, he roared, "Look what those sorry son-of-a-guns have done to Ringer!" You would have thought they had beaten up each player's grandmother. The room went nuts. Coach told his players that any team who had the audacity to rough up a poor defenseless dog would pay for it. Coach Teaff's outmanned McMurry team not only won the game but also set two records that night: The first was for turnovers caused, and the second was for personal fouls. Often, as leaders, we forget to nurture the art of motivation. If we want our spouses or children to do something, we gripe. Or pout. Or beg. Or explode in anger. That might get results for a while, but better in the long run is learning to motivate our families to be better and do better.

Great motivators like Coach Teaff create a positive atmosphere in their environment. They put their team, whether it's a sports team, a corporate team or a family, in a mental state that is conducive to achieving the greatest possible results. From time to time, you will find a leader who motivates with fear or by threatening his or her group, but most of the time you will find that leaders who motivate people to do amazing things are people whom other people want to be around and want to be like. Great motivators are positive and encouraging. What I have found, which constantly puzzles me, is that it is more challenging to motivate my own family than it is to motivate outsiders. I find it easy to encourage and energize people at church, in my work, and on teams I coach. But at home, I find it isn't so easy. At home, I'm more likely to see the glass as being half empty rather than half full. I find it easier to notice the one *B* on my son's report card than the five *A*s. I instruct the parents of my youth soccer team after a game, "Just tell your sons how you love watching them play. Don't talk about the game, especially their mistakes or effort." Yet I find myself fighting the urge to tell *my* son the things he did wrong. I am not saying we should never give constructive criticism, but there will be plenty of time for that later if it is needed. Encouraging our kids with the positive is usually far more effective than giving warnings about the negative.

Most of us are motivated by the promise of pleasure or the avoidance of pain. The avoidance of pain is a negative and emotionally draining motivation style, but the promise of pleasure is one that's positive. I can tell my son that if he doesn't mow the yard, he can't spend the night at his friend's house. Or, I can encourage him to get the yard mowed so he will be able to go spend the night with his friend. It's the same message, just in a different wrapper. Discipline is part of our family culture. And part of being disciplined is taking care of business before pleasure. I tell my family I want to bless them with freedoms that come from doing what they are supposed to do, and sleeping over at a friend's house is one of those freedoms.

Regardless of your natural emotional state, which might or might not be particularly optimistic, if you want to be a better motivator, be more positive. When I was in high school, I met a guy who practiced positive thinking. I found I liked being around that guy. Whenever anyone asked how he was doing, he always responded, "Terrific." I thought to myself, *I want to be terrific too*. I asked him how it was that he always felt terrific, and he laughed and said, "I don't always feel terrific, but I always answer that way because I find the more I say it, the more I believe it—and the more I believe it, the more I feel it." I adopted the *terrific* response and it works! Now don't get me wrong, I have bad days. But the first step to feeling positive is acting positive.

A story that has had a profound impact on me is about a boy who grew up in rural Mississippi back in the 1950s. His family had a farm and it was a lean season for them. Every morning, this boy's Momma woke him up early to go outside and do chores before the older kids would go off to school. She would always wake him up with a gentle touch and then say, "Time to get up. It's gonna be a good day today." The little boy would jump up and get on a stool in front of the wood-burning stove, and his Momma would pour him a little coffee with a lot of cream. He would sip that coffee in front of that warm stove while his Momma made breakfast.

One frigid Mississippi morning, his Momma came in to wake him, and she said, as she always did, "Time to get up. It's gonna be a good day today."

But it was extra cold on this day, and the boy had not slept so well. So he said, "No, it's not gonna be a good day today. It's gonna be a bad day," and he turned over and pulled the covers over his head. His Momma just turned around and walked out and went about her business. About an hour later, the little boy got up and lumbered into the kitchen, wrapped himself in his blanket, sat on the stool, and asked his Momma for his morning coffee.

His Momma said, "Ohhhh no, you made a choice this morning that it was gonna be a bad day, and it is gonna be a bad day all day long." She told her son to go get back in bed and said that he wasn't to get up all day.

About noon, the boy was bored and hungry, so he went into the kitchen, where his Momma reminded him again that he had chosen to have a bad day and that he was to go back to bed and have his bad day. He thought, *What kind of woman would make her son go hungry all day?* The older kids had gone off to school, and when they came home, the little boy could smell the fresh bread his Momma had made for a snack for them. By now his stomach was growling. He poked his head around the corner, but the look from his Momma was clear: The bread and hand-churned butter were not for him. The older kids ate their snack and went into the fields until dinner.

About 6 P.M., his Momma came in to check on her youngest son. She reminded him that in life we have to make the most of every day, and that sometimes we have to choose to have a good day even when our circumstances don't dictate it. She gave her son a sandwich and a glass of water; after he finished his supper, he stayed in bed and thought about what his Momma had said.

The next morning, his Momma came in to wake him up, and as always she said, "Time to get up. It's gonna be a good day today."

That boy jumped out of bed, rushed to his little stool, and said, "Yes, ma'am, it's gonna be a good day today." I heard this story 35 years ago, and I still think about it when I wake up and don't feel like it's gonna be a good day. I tell myself it *will* be and I start to program my subconscious to believe it. Then, when I wake my boys up, I tell them that I love them, that I am proud of them, and that it's gonna be a good day today.

Romans 8:28 says that no matter what is going on in your life, God can make it work for your good. If you believe that, you will not be able to help but be an encouragement to others. You will find that your life is better and you will find that more people want to be around you. Keep in mind that you aren't trying to change all the haters who will choose to have a bad day every day. You are just trying to start with your attitude and your family's attitude. If you do this, you will find that you can motivate those closest to you—and then together you can motivate others.

GamePlan

- Make a commitment to approach each day with a more hopeful attitude. You will find that the more positive you are, the easier it will be to be encouraging to others.

- Make a point of looking for the good in your family. List a few of the things you admire and appreciate about each of your family members. Share these at your next huddle. Mix up the constructive criticism with moments of pure praise and affirmation.

- Make note of the positive people in your life. How do their upbeat attitudes affect you? Make a point of spending time with them and emulating them.

- Look for the good in everyone you encounter. Make it a game; some people will make the game a challenge, but keep at it. As opportunities arise, share with them what you see. You'll be surprised by the impact your positive words can have on them.

20

Move Away from the Joneses

Jon Hesse arrived at the University of Nebraska in 1992 driving a four-year-old pickup truck. He was an All-Conference linebacker for the Cornhuskers' notorious Black Shirt Defense. The Jacksonville Jaguars selected Jon in the 1997 NFL draft. He rode into Jacksonville in the same old truck he'd driven onto the University of Nebraska campus. In a strange twist of fate, Jon spent all but three weeks of the 1997 season on the practice squad of the Green Bay Packers. The Denver Broncos signed him off the Packers' practice squad at the end of December, and Jon finished the season as a Super Bowl Champion when the Denver Broncos beat his former Green Bay Packer teammates in Super Bowl XXXII. And yes, he was still driving that old pickup.

Jon is a wise man. He understands that life in the NFL is tenuous at best. He could have afforded to buy a new truck along the way but decided to play it smart. It's no wonder that after his NFL career came to an end, he decided to go into the financial management business. He has been successful applying the same common sense tactics that served him so well with other NFL players and with individuals like you and me.

I have seen a lot of players take the exact opposite approach. Most rookie players sign a four-year contract. If drafted in the third through sixth rounds, they receive a signing bonus in the

$50,000 to $800,000 range. They have a first-year base salary in the $400,000 range, and a total base salary over the four years of roughly $2 million. The trick, though, is that if they don't make the team, the signing bonus is all they will see. A lot of players start counting on the whole contract from day one. To be successful, it is necessary for players to be confident that they will make the team, but it isn't wise for them to spend the money before they actually receive it.

One year, the Dallas Cowboys drafted two defensive backs in the fourth and sixths rounds, respectively. Both players showed up at the Cowboys facility in brand-new S-class Mercedes. The sixth-rounder supposedly purchased his prior to the draft in expectation of being a higher pick. Both players lasted two years and then both were cut. It is easy to understand why players can feel like they have found an actual money tree, especially the guys who sign big contracts. Players get paid every Tuesday during the season. They show up and pick up a check for $100,000 or $200,000 and they know that the next Tuesday they will get another one. A teammate buys a $50,000 watch, so they go buy a $60,000 one. Many players buy a house in their NFL city and a house in their off-season location. They have been told, probably by the realtor who sold them the house, that purchasing real estate is smarter than throwing money away on rent.

Dave Williams, of the San Diego Chargers, was riding with a teammate on their way to lunch one Tuesday. They had just picked up their checks, and Dave's friend drove by the Bentley dealership. The guy told Dave he had always wanted a Bentley and pulled into the dealership. He walked up to a jet-black convertible and announced to the salesman, who had not even had a chance to introduce himself, "I'll take this one." The price tag was $250,000. Dave asked his friend if he was going to go through with this purchase. The player pulled out his check, which was for $285,000. He concluded that he could live on the leftover $35,000 until he got another $285,000 check the following week. It is easy to feel rich when you look at it like that.

At Domann & Pittman, our motto is: "Pursue Excellence." But the goal isn't *just* to be excellent on the playing field. As agents, we strive to help our clients become the best players, teammates, employees, friends, fathers, sons and husbands they can be. We take a keen interest in the personal development of our clients. Among other things, this means helping them properly steward the money they earn while they play professionally. I often tell my players, "You can live like a king for a few years or you can live like a prince forever. The choice is yours."

Just like the rest of us, football players are surrounded by people who always seem to have more than they do. And, as it does for us, this stirs in them a desire to live beyond their means—a habit that can have catastrophic long-term effects. A successful family will learn to manage their finances well in order to build an environment of stability and establish a secure future. No one likes to diet and no one likes to budget, but healthy spending habits are as important to our well-being as healthy eating habits are. The dictionary defines "austerity" as the trait of great self-denial, especially refraining from worldly pleasures. Sounds fun, huh? You're probably tempted to skip the rest of this chapter, but please don't; as you read on, it will make sense.

One of the dangers of living in the "greatest nation in the world" is that it's easy to believe the hype. Here's the headline: "Everyone deserves more—and while it may look like you can't afford it, you actually can." Yeah, right! One character trait I try to develop in my clients is the ability to ignore the hype—both the good and the bad. I tell them, "You are never as *good* as the press and fans say you are, and you are never as *bad* as they say you are." The hype in America has been that we all deserve a bigger house, a pool, a boat and a new car. But just because the realtor and mortgage broker say you can—and should—have the house you never thought you could afford, this isn't necessarily true. Our government isn't a good example either. It doesn't operate according to sound financial principles. If we operated our finances like the government does, we'd all be in jail. Our whole nation has become so dependent on credit, to pay for a lifestyle we can't afford, that our country is sinking.

Have you fallen into that trap? If you have, now is the time to change. If you haven't, don't buy into the hype. Once you fall into that pit, it's hard to get out. One of my clients, Antonio Johnson, had driven the same truck since he'd entered the league as a fourth-round pick. He'd been smart and waited until after the draft to get it. He didn't go crazy and buy a Land Rover or Mercedes. He bought a dependable truck, put some nice wheels on it, and added a bangin' sound system. I was proud of him. After his third year in the league, he told me he wanted to get a Navigator. I said okay, and then asked if he was going to trade in the truck, which was paid off. He informed me that he wanted to keep the truck. I did some calculations and showed him that if he made a reasonable down payment and financed the Navigator for four years, he would pay about $20,000 more than the sticker price by the time all was said and done. I also showed him that if he put the same amount in an investment account and left it there for 20 years, he would have about $150,000. So, all told, the new vehicle would cost him about $220,000. He decided against the purchase and invested that money instead. Even though he played a few more years, he was happy he had saved the money when he set out to start his own company after his playing days were over.

My wife's grandfather lived 94 years and never made a lot of money. He lived by a simple rule: If you can't afford it, don't buy it. He paid cash for everything, even his house. He never once owed anybody anything. He shared some valuable wisdom with me before he passed away. He told me about an article he'd read on creative financing. His take on it was interesting: If you have to have creative financing for something, you probably can't afford it.

I remember going out to play golf at a great course in a new housing community outside of Dallas. I was pretty new in my profession and had not yet turned the corner, so money was tight. The course was beautiful and was lined with huge, lavishly appointed homes.

I asked my buddy, "Who lives in these homes and what the heck do they do for a living?"

My friend laughed and said, "The people who live there don't own those homes; the banks do." He went on to surmise that the cars were leased, the boats were financed, and these people would be in big-time trouble if the next raise didn't come through or if the economy slipped. We all know that the economy *did* slip— some would say it was more of a free-fall—caused in large part by the mortgage crisis. Foreclosures and bankruptcies hit all-time highs. The advice of my 94-year-old grandfather-in-law would have saved a lot of people a lot of heartache. I have a friend who shared *his* grandfather's key to being rich. It went like this: "Old car, old house, old wife." Seems like these older guys have a lot of wisdom for our generation.

The Bible tells us to be lenders, not borrowers. It continues on to compare the lender to the *head* and the borrower to the *tail* (see Deut. 28:12-13). That is a perspective that is pretty easy to comprehend. I know which end I would rather be.

Another good principle is to give the first 10 percent of your income to the Lord. This is called a *tithe*. Put the next 10 percent in savings. If you can't live on 80 percent of your income, you are probably living a lifestyle you can't afford. I wish I could say that I learned this principle early on in life and have practiced it for as long as I can remember. That is not the case. I am as guilty as the next guy. But I am leading a household, and it is my responsibility to practice sound financial principles. I am the risk-taker in my house and the one who needs to be held in check. Thankfully, God has given me a prudent wife who is more risk-averse than I am, which makes us a good team.

I also encourage you to make big financial decisions as a team. Always include your wife, and do your best to include your kids as well. The extent to which you include them will depend on their ages. Remember, you are a leader, not a dictator. Teach your kids sound financial principles by showing them why you shouldn't put in that pool by taking out a home equity loan. If you run up credit card debt, fail to plan for retirement, fail to save for their college tuition, live month-to-month and some months come up short, you will likely have kids who do the same thing. I doubt that's the legacy you want to leave.

One mark of the socio-economic culture in America is that many of us try to "keep up with the Joneses." I say, *Move away from the Joneses!* They are probably going to get their house repossessed anyway. Make sure your family understands that a person's value has nothing to do with his or her net worth or earning capacity. It is far more important to live a life of character and integrity than it is to have a big bank account.

GamePlan

- Live within your means. Put together a household budget, then stay within that budget. Do not use credit cards to improve your lifestyle.

- If you are already in debt, do everything you can to get out. This might involve getting into a program like the one offered by Dave Ramsey. Talk with your wife and kids about the family's financial situation, and seek their input and support to make changes.

- Practice the "old car, old house, old wife" principle. If this is an area of struggle for you, ask God to help you and find someone you trust to hold you accountable.

- Practice the "live on 80 percent" principle. Re-evaluate your budget and spending habits. What can you do to give back to God and to prepare for your future?

- Teach your kids sound financial principles. Talk with your kids about giving, saving, and other financial habits. Help them come up with plans for how they will handle their money.

21

Keep Dreaming

Playing in the NFL has been called "living the dream." So what does one do as an encore when that dream is over? Players who have no dreams beyond professional football sometimes slide into a tailspin after they leave the league. That's why I always encourage my players to start thinking about their post-NFL aspirations early on in their playing careers. Too often, these young men haven't thought about much more than football, because football was the dream and they achieved it! It's hard to get 24- or 25-year-old guys to realize that their football careers are going to come to an end. They've spent their whole lives getting there, so focusing on the dream ending isn't something they are inclined to do. But unlike a lot of sports agents, I don't have many players who leave the league feeling lost. That's because I have learned the value of dreaming *beyond* the NFL, and I instill this value in my clients while they're still playing.

Similarly, your family is fueled by dreams. As with my players, your wife has—or deserves to have!—dreams beyond changing diapers and giving baths. Even if she chooses to stay at home with the children, she should be given the space and resources to pursue her other dreams as well. This could mean different things for different women. My wife wanted to be able to do the homeroom mom thing and go have lunch with the boys at school, but she wanted to work her business a little too. As a leader, it is up to you to make sure your wife doesn't feel trapped or stifled. Is it her dream to be a stay-at-home mom, or is that your dream for her? Likewise, you may work a 9-to-5 job that isn't your dream job, and you may be glad to do so for the sake of supporting your family, but that doesn't mean you should stop developing and pursuing your dreams. One of my dreams was to be involved in developing the men's ministry in my church. Several years ago, God gave me the dream to write a book. Kids are natural dreamers, but often as parents we don't fan these flames in their hearts, and the dreams flicker until they have faded away. Don't let this happen in your family. Everyone deserves to dream.

I remember talking to one of my high school teachers about what I wanted to do after I graduated. After hearing my plans to be a professional soccer player and to play in Europe, this teacher told me I was dreaming. But by "dreaming," what he actually meant was "unrealistic." Looking back, I understand why he said it. The plans were extravagant, at the least, and possibly a little crazy. At first, when he called me a dreamer, I was *proud* of the label. Then I noticed his countenance. He meant it in a bad way. I didn't understand why it would be silly to dream and dream big. I admit, the dreams I had in high school didn't come to pass, but I didn't stop dreaming. I just dreamed new dreams when it became obvious the old dreams were not a part of God's plan.

Just as there are those who try to moderate young people's dreams, so too the same can be true in adulthood. When I started my company, the head football coach at a major university told me I'd never make it. He wasn't trying to squelch my dream and he wasn't being mean. But he knew I would follow the rules, and he thought that would put me at such a disadvantage that I would never be able to compete. Some agents offer large sums of money to entice players to sign with them. Others arrange for players to receive expensive cars, computers, watches, custom-made suits, you name it. I told him I thought he was wrong—not about my following the rules, but about my not being able to make it. Then, after three years of struggling and barely getting by, seeing other agents doing things I wouldn't do, I started to think that maybe he was right. But God had given me the vision and the dream to be a sports agent, so I clung to the conviction that He was going to see it through.

In Acts 2:17, Paul quotes the prophet Joel, saying, "In the last days, God says, I will pour out my Spirit on all people. Your sons and daughters will prophesy, your young men will see visions, your old men will dream dreams" (*NIV*). This is a great message for you as the leader of your home. First of all, how cool is it that God will pour out His Spirit on us? Now, when God pours His Spirit out on us, we still have to choose how we are going to respond. We don't come under some God-forced mind control. We have to move on what the Spirit leads us to do. Second, even cooler than God doing a work in *my* life, God is doing a work in my wife's life and in my kids' lives. To think of my sons prophesying is an awesome thought. To think of my sons having Holy Spirit-inspired visions born of prophetic inspiration is exciting. Finally, I like the promise that I will still be able to participate by dreaming dreams even when I am old.

If you are skeptical by nature, or are not a natural dreamer, let this verse inspire you. Think about the advantages of buying into a Spirit-led, prophetic, visions and dreams-type life! I am a dreamer. My parents always encouraged me to think big, and they instilled the "you can do anything you set your mind to" mentality in me. From the time I was six years old, I wanted to be a professional athlete. At first I wanted to be an NFL player; I grew up in Dallas and aspired to be a Dallas Cowboy. While playing, I pretended I was Roger Staubach, Cliff Harris or Drew Pearson. Then I went through my basketball stage, during which I planned to go to UCLA and play for the legendary John Wooden. Later, when soccer became my passion, I planned to go to Europe and play in the English Premier League. Perhaps hearing my childhood dreams has you thinking about your own. For some reason, we behave as if it's okay to dream as a child but it's not acceptable to have dreams as a man. We think that when we grow up we have to settle for less. Why is that?

When I told my parents I was going to play for the Dallas Cowboys, they didn't cite the statistics that only a small percentage of people end up playing in the NFL, or even going on to play college football. No, they encouraged me and told me that if I was going to be the best, I had to work hard. They knew God had a plan for my life and that He had given me abilities that would mold my dreams. They knew my desires would adapt and I would settle into my sweet spot.

So many adults have been beaten down by life, and by their inability to achieve their own dreams, that they crush their children's dreams without even realizing it. I hear adults justifying their dream-crushing—perhaps dissuading a child who wants to be a singing sensation—by claiming that they don't want their kids to get *hurt*. But which is worse for a child: realizing they're not the country's greatest musical talent or being trained to settle for less?

The number one cause of "dead dreams" is theft. That's right. The Bible states that we have an enemy (see 1 Pet. 5:8). In John 10:10, Jesus explains that our enemy wants to kill, steal and destroy. But the Bible also states that we have power over the enemy (see Luke 10:19 and 1 John 4:4). When it came to my dream of working as an agent, it was amazing how often the enemy came in and tried to steal it! There were countless stumbling blocks in the form of missed clients, stolen clients, being stood up by prospects, injuries to clients, and poor play by other clients. But God had given me the dream and that kept me in the game.

Your role as a leader is to learn how to dream Spirit-led dreams and guide your family to do the same. God does not tell us He is going to take away the obstacles or prevent every attack of the enemy. He does tell us He will see us through the hard times. So many people get discouraged fighting off the enemy and they quit. I admit it can get tiring when you are constantly being attacked, but if you keep your eyes on Jesus, you will be able to persevere. The enemy's strategy is to discourage us to the point that we give up.

I have found two critical factors in maintaining one's ability to keep dreaming. First, you have to let go of the wheel and let God drive the bus. Our dreams need to be developed and shaped by God. God has a plan for our lives, so we need to realize that our dreams may start off looking one way but may end up looking a little different as He shapes them. I love Ephesians 1:17-19 in relation to this thought. As we gain the spirit of wisdom and revelation in the knowledge of God, our eyes and hearts will be enlightened and we will become keenly aware of what God has called us to. Paul goes on in verse 19 to remind us that we have the immeasurable greatness of His power. What an encouragement.

Second, we have to be willing to call audibles. When what we thought was the dream gets crushed, we have to be in close fellowship with the Father and say, "Okay, now what does my dream look like?" Sometimes a dream ends because we were following our own dreams versus following God's leading. Sometimes experiencing some failure is part of reaching the dream. Everything worth attaining is going to be difficult and there will be plenty of obstacles. We have to press on and call an audible when we feel God leading us to change the course a little. I have heard that many great inventions were discovered "by accident." A scientist was working toward one thing and, in the process, found something else that changed the world. Every failure should be viewed as a step closer to victory and a lesson in what isn't part of our dream.

One of the attributes of a great leader is the ability to get people to be their best. If you are going to be a great leader in your home, you will help your spouse and your children accomplish their dreams. A common misstep in this area is when parents try to accomplish their kids' dreams *for* them. Your role is to encourage dreaming and to facilitate the pursuit of dreams. When members of your family hit stumbling blocks, you can help them assess the obstacles and brainstorm solutions. You don't have to solve all your family's problems for them—nor should you. I confess, this is a challenge for me. I don't like seeing those I love struggling. I want to get in there and fix things for them! But if I solve the problems, they don't learn how to—and they don't get the satisfaction that comes from figuring out their own solutions.

Finally, let your family members have their own dreams. Do everything you can to avoid pushing your dreams on your family. You probably know some dads who impose their dreams on their kids.

ESPN produced a documentary on Todd Marinovich, the outstanding QB of the USC Trojans and Oakland Raiders. Todd's father, Marv Marinovich, started training Todd to be a professional football player from the day he was born. Marv said that while Todd was in the crib, he would stretch his little legs—and when he could only crawl, he would have him crawl hundreds of yards as a workout. As Todd got a bit older, he said he *chose* to be "trained" by his father to be a professional QB. What else was he going to say? It was his *dad*. But Todd ended up despising football, and he asked the question "Just because you are gifted to be something, does it mean that is what you are supposed to be?" I would say the answer is maybe, but maybe not. What is your Holy Spirit-inspired dream? If it is to be a professional QB, then great—but if it isn't, then fulfilling that role will not satisfy you. I am not passing judgment on the Marinoviches. Both Marv and Todd did what they felt was best at the time. Both were candid in the film, admitting that, in hindsight, they'd both made mistakes. Their story, sadly, is more common than we think.

Develop a culture of dreaming in your home. Holy Spirit-inspired dreams are the key to finding fulfillment in your life. Help your family shape their dreams and encourage them to recalculate when a dream is unfulfilled.

When I was young, I just knew I was going to be a professional athlete. Ultimately, I was not gifted enough as an athlete to play professionally, but my love of sports and the ability to play at a high level were part of my preparation for my God-given purpose of being a sports agent. Because I was encouraged to dream, I now have my dream wife, my dream job and my dream life.

GamePlan

- If you are not a dreamer by nature, start to change your mindset. Allow the possibility that your Spirit-led dreams can come true. What were your passions and interests as a young person? Is there something new that is tugging at your heart?

- Be prayerful that God will give you dreams and the Holy Spirit will give you the wisdom to act on His prompting. Ask God what dreams He has for you, and what the first step is that you should take in moving toward it.

- Understand that you have an enemy who wants to steal your dreams. Protect your dreams by staying in fellowship with Christ and with people who support you.

- Don't get discouraged; don't give up! Do pray for wisdom and allow God to reshape your dreams if necessary.

- Don't allow your past experiences to negatively influence your family's dreams. How can you be more supportive of your family's dreams going forward?

- Don't push your dreams on your family. Are there things you never accomplished that you pressure your children to do? How can you free each member of the family to go after his or her own dreams?

22

Encourage Creativity

In 1971, when Bill Arnsparger was the defensive coordinator for the Miami Dolphins, no one knew what a zone blitz was. Coach Arnsparger started lining up extra defensive linemen and dropping one or more into coverage. Dick LeBeau picked up on this tactic in the early '90s, and some would say that, as the defensive coordinator for the Pittsburgh Steelers, he perfected it. The Steelers became known as *Blitzburgh*. These days, not only is the tactic commonplace, but also several variations of the zone blitz have been created.

If one team finds success doing something, suddenly everyone else is doing it too.

For the first 30 years of the modern NFL era, teams worked to establish the running game at all costs. Then along came a coach named Bill Walsh, in the mid 1980s, who dismissed the run in favor of a short passing game. The West Coast offense was born and took the NFL by storm. Bill Parcells is credited with coining the term. His New York Giants were matched against the high-flying San Francisco 49ers in an NFC playoff game. Parcells was known for tough defense, while the 49ers were being touted as potentially unstoppable. The Giants emerged victorious, 17-3, and Parcells said in his post-game press conference, "What do you think of that West Coast Offense now?"[1] In the decades since its invention, many great coaches have employed the system, including Mike Holmgren, Steve Mariucci, Andy Reid, Jim Fassel and Brian Billick.

The current craze in both college football and the NFL is the *up tempo* offensive schemes run by Chip Kelly, Gus Malzahn, Urban

Meyer and Art Briles. Even in a game with strict rules, creativity is rewarded, and the pioneers of these innovations achieve success.

I have applied this principle in my home, encouraging my children to try new things and to test the limits of possibility, even though creativity is not something that comes naturally to me. Layne, on the other hand, is crazy creative. I appreciate that gift in her; for my part, I just figure that if something isn't natural, it doesn't mean it's impossible—it just needs to be developed. Whether it is writing music or selling shoes made of duct tape to other kids at school, I have attempted to light a spark in my children to create greater creativity and increased enthusiasm for life.

Yes, that's right—I said duct tape shoes.

Eli came out of school one day and convinced his mom that they needed to go to the hardware store to get some duct tape. Layne inquired if it was for a school project; Eli just said he had an idea. This is where Layne deserves kudos. I probably would have shut it down, but she went with it. They came home with a roll of pink duct tape and a roll of camouflage duct tape. Eli took some Styrofoam that we had left over from a previous school project and drew around his foot. He cut out the shape and covered it in duct tape, with a band going over the top to secure the shoe to his foot. He had made a pair of duct tape slides.

He wore them to school the next day, and when Layne picked him up, he informed her that he needed to go back to the hardware store for a few more rolls of duct tape. Layne asked why, and he told her he had sold five pairs of slides: two pink and three camo. He already had the money. When we asked how he knew what size to make the shoes, he showed us a piece of paper with a tracing of each kid's foot! Eli ended up selling 15 pairs of slides before the project was scrapped because the production was eating into his chill time. I must admit, I was a proud daddy.

Yet despite such compelling evidence, I still struggle with the temptation to put a damper on my family's creativity. Naturally, I am just more comfortable coloring inside the lines. I like order and discipline. I like to find the best way to do something and then do it that way all the time. Layne is different. She will do the same activity differently every time, just because she enjoys seeing the different ways to do things. She has helped me appreciate the benefits of getting outside the box, and I've actually found even better ways of doing a few things by trying different options. I do not think there is a right and a wrong here—just various preferences—but there is definitely value in developing the ability to think differently and learning to be open-minded in certain areas. For example, you may typically choose the fastest and most direct way to the grocery store, and that's great for efficiency's sake, but it might do you good to consider taking the scenic route every now and then. By taking the scenic route you may find a better way or you may learn to enjoy something different. You may even find it makes you appreciate the norm even more.

Creativity is not confined to the arts. When we encourage creativity in a variety of areas, our children learn how to be innovative and become better problem solvers. They generate new ideas and build on existing ones. Professor Robert Fisher writes about developing creative thinking and expanding the minds of young learners. He defines creativity as "applying imagination and looking for alternative innovative outcomes in any activity."[2] I like the fact that my wife is helping all of her boys—me included—to view the world in a different way. When we tend toward using the more logical left side of our brains, she encourages us to use the more creative right side.

Of course, there is a difference between exploring the creative and being shaped by other people's creativity. I think this happens when a family isn't well grounded. It also happens when our children's creativity is left to others. For example, when our kids lose themselves in certain video games, I believe they miss out on opportunities to be truly creative. As parents, we are responsible for developing and guiding our children's creativity rather than leaving it in the hands of others. Reading aloud to your kids from quality literature, working together to create something in your yard (a garden, a fort, a sculpture out of found objects), and attending a live music or drama performance are all ways to inspire creativity.

A sense of humor is one form of creativity. I heard somebody say that they give their kids the task of finding a funny joke and telling it to the whole family every evening at dinner. I've heard humor is something that can be developed, like biceps, and I've also heard that a good sense of humor is a sign of intelligence. Either way, I don't know many people who don't like to laugh. Humor and creativity have been linked with joy, self-confidence and an easy-going nature. So to promote humor is a good way to develop creativity and other great personality traits. Part of my family's current plan to grow creatively together is to establish a joke night. I'm thinking about an award that can be passed around from week to week to recognize the funniest joke or story.

Around the time our boys were born, many experts were recommending listening to classical music with young children. Some research had concluded that this helped children develop and possibly improved their intelligence. Since my kids were stuck with a lot of my DNA, I figured they would need all the help they could get. So we tried it. I don't know if it helped with their intelligence or not, but I do know that when Jake was a baby, and we were driving to see relatives, there were times when we wouldn't have made it without the music, because he would cry non-stop unless Mozart or Bach was playing. We also learned that infants could be taught sign language before they could speak. Teaching our sons sign language was a creative strategy that reduced both boys' frustration levels, along with ours. Instead of not knowing how to communicate with us, they used sign language. Another way to encourage creativity is to throw out a riddle in the morning and see who can figure it out by dinner. I encourage you to do some research and find ways to help develop creativity in your children, your wife and yourself.

I am convinced that creative, innovative, problem-solving kids will be more self-confident, joyful and successful. For that matter, most parents can afford to expand our creativity and enjoy some of these benefits as well.

GamePlan

- Evaluate your creativity factor. If it is low, find some ways to develop it: Take a different route to your usual destinations. Find a new solution to an old problem. Take up a new hobby.

- Encourage creativity in your children and in your wife. Perhaps your family can brainstorm new ways to liven up a familiar routine or event.

- Discuss as a family ways you can all grow your creative muscle together. Whether it's family talent nights or a new schedule of chores, your family will draw closer together and create fun memories for everyone.

Notes

1. David Harris, *The Genius: How Bill Walsh Reinvented Football and Created an NFL Dynasty* (New York: Random House, 2009), p. 249.
2. Robert Fisher, "Expanding Minds: Developing Creative Thinking in Young Learners," *CATS: The IATEFL Young Learners SIG Journal,* Spring 2006, pp. 5-9.

23

Clean Out Your Closet

In the early '90s, I represented Tyson Henson, a running back for the Atlanta Falcons. Though he wasn't living the NFL "life"—a wild and crazy, party-'til-you-drop lifestyle—he knew he needed to cut out some destructive habits.

Tyson was still dating his college girlfriend. During his rookie year, she was finishing school while he was trying to make it in the NFL as an undrafted free agent. That year, Tyson had his share of fun times with the boys at the clubs. There were plenty of available girls, and commitment was not in his vocabulary. His second season brought about a change in his living arrangements, and subsequently his party habits, when his girlfriend graduated and moved in with him. Gone were the days of runnin' the clubs with his boys. Then the big change happened.

About halfway through that second season, I was changing planes in the Tulsa airport. The call came while I was hurrying from one gate to the next. It was Tyson.

"I just had to call and tell you that I accepted Christ today and my life is different," he informed me.

I stopped dead in my tracks. It took me a moment to process the information and another to get the words out. But I did get them out.

"That is *awesome!*" I screamed as other passengers stopped and stared at me.

Tyson then said that he knew he needed to "clean out his closet." He proposed to his girlfriend and committed to kicking all the bad habits that were inconsistent with the new Tyson. He didn't want to be like so many other players who had been dragged down by the secrets in their lives.

Nothing will destroy a family faster than a secret or a "hidden" habit. Whether it is a little lie about money or a big lie about an affair, bad behavior practiced in secret will erode the foundations of a family. Most of us hold on to some habit we know isn't good for us at some point in our lives. If you haven't cleaned out your closet in a while, you probably should.

I was saved by Christ when I was 13 years old. But I didn't change my lifestyle significantly until I was 25. Even then, the change was gradual. I had certain habits and behaviors I didn't want to give up. By the time I was 30, I was nowhere near perfect—and still am not—but I had taken out most of the trash of my life. I had stopped hanging around certain friends. I was going to church. I'd learned how to pray, and I was consistent in my study of God's Word. If my walk with Christ was a *house*, it was pretty darn clean—*except* for the corner of that closet in the back room. I was still holding on to a few things and storing them there.

It's like the story of the man holding a gallon of cool, crystal-clear water in the middle of a hot summer day. He asks the crowd if anyone would like a drink. Everyone responds that they would love a drink. The man then pours a thimbleful of raw sewage into the gallon of pure water and, suddenly, he has no takers. Your life and my life can look like that if we don't clean out our closets and let go of all the junk we've collected.

This is a tough area for most men to address. While we become new creations when we accept Christ, we still have a sinful nature. I wish God had made part of the "new creation" thing the complete removal of any desire to sin. I wish my flesh didn't want so many carnal things. I wish my new spirit were completely void of selfishness. Unfortunately, the things of the world are still appealing to my flesh. I still love myself more than I love others. I still have anger and rage that can pop up without warning. I guess overcoming these traits is part of the process of becoming more like Christ. The Word tells us that if we resist the enemy, he will flee from us (see Jas. 4:7). The hard part is that sometimes the resisting takes awhile.

I want you to be encouraged, and you should be. That said, removing sin is tough. Even though you desire to grow in Christ and want to be a better husband and dad, you might also have a desire to hang on to that *one thing* that feeds your flesh. Or you may not *want* to hold on to it at all, but you can't seem to get rid of it. Here's what I know: There are too many men going to church, treating their wives well, being there for their kids, and struggling privately with something that feels bigger than them.

I've been there, hanging on to some things that I knew God wanted out of my life. I had a 20-year snuff habit. When I got back into the church and started to understand how to get closer to God and how to listen to the Holy Spirit, I began to make changes in my life. God was working on me, and I made drastic, radical changes in my thinking, my behaviors and my overall way of life. But I held on to a few things, and one of them was my snuff. I even met the woman of my dreams—my wife, Layne—and kept on dipping. Not in front of her, of course, but I kept on dipping.

I thought, *I have given up almost all of my bad habits, and God doesn't expect me to be perfect, and I am such a better man than I have ever been. Certainly this one thing won't be too bad.*

Sound familiar?

But one day I finally opened my ears and heard the Holy Spirit say, "This isn't My best for you. This isn't what I want for you. Your body is My temple, where I reside. Don't treat it like that." So I stopped.

I knew God had called me to obedience, and that if I gave my addiction to Him, He would help me get through it. I wish I could say I lost the craving for snuff in a miraculous way and never had the desire to dip again. But that wasn't the case. I had strong cravings for it for years. I believe that when we become children of God, He walks with us, encourages us, and wants His best for us. The process of removing sin from our lives is not fast or easy, but God will stay with us as we work our way through it.

I don't know what you're hiding. Maybe you have been down this road already and have cleaned out your closet. If so, that's great. But if you are still holding on to something, let it go.

From the beginning of time, men have been so strong and yet so weak. Just look at Adam. How about Samson? David? Peter? Paul?

No one likes to admit to weakness, so we make excuses. I know some awesome, godly men who have terrible tempers. There are men leading Bible studies who can't let a woman walk by without checking her out. There are men in the next pew who struggle with alcohol on a daily basis. And what about pornography? It didn't get to be the gazillion-dollar industry it is without luring in some Christian men.

The enemy will tell you that you're okay—that you don't need to worry about that *one* little thing. But a thimbleful of sin in the pure water of your soul will contaminate your whole being and keep you from becoming all God has designed you to be. Clean out your closet and enjoy the freedom God desires for you.

GamePlan

- Identify the things you are holding on to, and admit to yourself that you have to get rid of them. Be prayerful and be honest with yourself.

- Get with a trusted Christian brother and share your struggle with him. Create an accountability system to keep yourself on track, and then follow through.

- We often try to hide our struggles from God, even though that is impossible. Be honest with God and thank Him for the victories—big and small—that He helps you to achieve.

- Don't listen to the devil. He will lie to you, telling you that either it's not that bad or that it's so bad you can't go back. Turn to Scripture to remind yourself of the truth: that God's grace is sufficient (see 2 Cor. 12:9), and that He will continue the good work He has begun in you (see Phil. 1:6).

24

Be Balanced

In 2004, I closed what may have been one of the fastest deals in recent NFL history. I had a cornerback who had been drafted by the Arizona Cardinals in 2000. He'd been an All-Conference player for a major university and had played in the Senior Bowl. After four years with the Cardinals, he was an unrestricted free agent and was making over a million dollars a year.

His contract expired on the last day of February and free agency began in March. I compiled a list of other free agents in the league, analyzed which teams had a strong need at his position, and began preliminary talks with teams to see who might consider signing him. One of my goals as an agent—in addition to getting my players the largest possible paycheck—is to match the player's personality with the team and the coaching staff.

After sizing up the situation, I knew it would come down to the Lions, Dolphins, Vikings and Jets. Each team needed to shore up their secondary, and I was one of the few agents who had a top-tier free agent at cornerback. I picked up the phone and called the general manager of one the teams. When he answered, I laid out my case for why this particular player was right for his team. The amount of money I was asking for would have made him the second-highest-paid cornerback in the NFL. The GM asked if I believed my client was the second-best cornerback in the league.

I replied, "He doesn't have to be the best. He just has to be the best *available*."

The general manager knew I was right. He could spend less, but the drop-off in talent would be unacceptable. In order to be successful, a team must be sound in all three phases of the game: offense, defense and special teams. Unfortunately, his team was imbalanced. They finished in the top 10 in five separate offensive categories, and did a solid job stopping the run on defense. They had the third-best punter in the league and the eighth-best kicker. But they needed to shore up their secondary. It was the one missing puzzle piece. As a result, I closed the deal—a $21 million contract that would have normally taken days to iron out—in only five minutes.

Too many people are like that team: effective or even exceptional in many areas but imbalanced overall. They may be financially prosperous but spiritually deprived. Or they might be socially active but have a broken marriage relationship. As in sports, we must learn to achieve balance—with our relationships, physical health, spiritual life and careers.

————|||||||————

When I was growing up, my father was the president and chairman of the board of a bank. I witnessed firsthand how difficult it can be to keep your finger on the pulse of your business *and* maintain a healthy balance with your family. That my parents were divorced made it even more complicated for my dad. But to his credit, he rose to the challenge. He was always involved in my sister's life and mine. He came to my games and my sister's dance recitals. I know now that it wasn't easy on him, but at the time he made it look that way.

I was blessed that even though my parents divorced, they did a great job of working together to make sure the collateral damage to us was kept at a minimum. Another blessing was that when my mom remarried, she found an awesome man to spend the rest of her life with. My stepdad had a juggling act of his own to manage: He had three boys from his first marriage and, of course, two stepchildren in my sister and me. He had to figure out how to balance having responsibility for five kids, three of whom did not live with him full-time. He was in semi-conductor sales for Texas Instruments, so work also had to be factored into the balancing act. I am thankful for the impact he has had on my life, and for the perspective I gleaned from both my dad and my stepdad.

As a sports agent, I could increase the number of nights I spend in hotels and days I spend on college campuses or in NFL cities. If I did, I would bring home a larger paycheck, but my family life would be strained. There is no replacement for time. We all have to make decisions regarding where our time should be spent. My wife and I decided that we would rather sacrifice a little professional success for our family than sacrifice our family for a little professional success. That was part of our thinking when we moved from Dallas to Salado. The slower pace would allow us to spend more quality time together as a family. With a heavy dose of hard work, we've been able to create a balanced household.

My partner, Craig Domann, and I have had many conversations about how to remain relevant in an industry that is incredibly time intensive and still maintain the balance we desire. I credit Craig with being a solid anchor in our business. Since the beginning, he has been consistent in striving for excellence and pushing for balance. In the early years of our partnership, we both were starting families, although he had a little bit of a head start on me there, and we both wanted to be great husbands and great dads. We were at an NFL game together one weekend, and after the game we ran into the GM of the team. He commented that it was good to see us and that our clients on his team were doing well. He then made an off-the-cuff statement about one of our competitors that confirmed our decision to seek balance. He mentioned that he saw us a few times a year, unlike the competitor, who was always there or somewhere else seeing games, clients or prospective clients. "But you guys probably know your wife and kids, and I know for a fact he doesn't," the GM commented. God has blessed us for not trying to "take over the world." We have a great business, and we have the opportunity to know our clients on a personal level.

Before I had children, I dreamed about building a dynasty. I thought about how cool my kids would think I was if I could leave them a huge sports agency business. I took my older son to a Houston Texans game versus the Kansas City Chiefs when he was eight years old. We went on the field and I introduced him to players, general managers, and even Bob McNair, the owner of the Texans. All he wanted to do was go to our seats and get some chicken fingers. My boys don't care what I do. They want to spend time with me. My wife doesn't value me according to how big I can make our bank account. She wants to share her life with me. I am committed to teaching my boys how to be real men—godly men of character and integrity—rather than teaching them that their value comes from their business success. I want to teach my boys how to love and respect their future wives by loving and respecting their mother. I want to teach them that it is better to drive an old car with your family in it to an old lake house for vacation than it is to fly in a private jet by yourself to some exotic resort. I would rather check in on the elderly widow in the neighborhood who needs her yard mowed and mow it for her than write a big check to some charity so I can get my name on a plaque. If I can teach my kids these values, then they can teach their kids. Remember, your kids may not act like they are paying attention or even like they care about the things you are teaching them. My boys are world champion eye-rollers when it comes to just about everything I say that is of long-term value. I get a lot of "I know, I know." But my years of volunteering in youth ministry taught me to be consistent and not to get discouraged—because it is sinking in, even when it seems like nothing is getting through.

Imbalanced parents often produce imbalanced children. If our children are good at music, we tend to push them harder, encouraging them to spend countless hours with instruments and iPods. If they are good at sports, we often sign them up for every season available, filling their schedules with practices, games and tournaments. And, yes, we can even be imbalanced spiritually. Parents can push their children to attend church every time the doors open, leaving little time to develop other facets of their lives.

Layne and I have identified the following aspects of life as critically important for our family: social life, sports and the arts, business, faith, family time, free time and education. We map out the time we're spending on each of these areas so that nothing gets overlooked or dominates the others. Why would my wife and I invest the requisite time in an activity that sounds about as fun as planning a financial budget? Because we recognize that we are responsible for helping to guide our children into healthier, more balanced rhythms.

As parents, this begins with us. Layne and I must model stability and balance for our children. A "do as I say, not as I do" strategy for parenting will not work. Once we have achieved balance in our own lives, we should assist our kids in implementing thoughtful schedules so that they won't wake up one day and realize they have a gaping hole that needs filling. If we can help children grow into well-balanced adults who live well-balanced lives, then we'll open up doors for them that might otherwise be closed.

GamePlan

- Do a bank account audit. What are you spending most of your money on? This is often a good indicator of balance or imbalance in your life.

- Take a look at your calendar. What is dominating your time? This is a good indication of balance or imbalance.

- Huddle up with your family to discuss areas that have become imbalanced—include your review of your finances and time. Give everyone the chance to assess the other members as well as themselves, and avoid the temptation to get defensive.

- As a family, brainstorm ways you can improve balance in your individual lives and in your life together. How can you support each other in striving for balance? Then agree to keep each other accountable.

25

Surround Yourself with Good Teammates

My client Kelvin Garmon ("KG" for short) was drafted by the Dallas Cowboys in 1999. That same year, the Cowboys drafted another talented player, Jerry Simpson. The two young teammates became good friends. Simpson was funny and just a good guy to be around—except that he didn't have a great work ethic and he was irresponsible. That season, KG came to understand the meaning of guilt by association. I finally had to advise him to distance himself from Simpson, as the Cowboys' coaches started thinking KG was involved in everything his friend did. To be completely honest, Simpson's poor work ethic and irresponsible behavior *was* causing KG to change, and not for the better.

I always encourage my rookie clients to find some veteran players to link up with, because that's the best way to learn the system, the nuances of the coaching staff, the game and their position. Specifically, I told KG to spend time with some veteran players who had the respect of the coaches—guys like Larry Allen, Erik Williams and Flozell Adams. KG identified Larry Allen as the guy he could learn from and who could help him earn the respect of the other veteran players and the coaches.

Larry Allen was a second-round draft pick from a tiny school called Sonoma State University. I had attended the East-West Shrine game on the Stanford University campus in Palo Alto, California, about five years earlier. The scouts were talking then about this small-school kid who was going to be the talk of the draft by the time draft weekend rolled around. Scouts always call players *kids*, but Larry Allen was actually a mountain of a man! He was already a five-time Pro Bowler when KG started hanging out with him. The interesting thing is that Simpson eventually started hanging out with KG and Larry Allen, and both rookie players became better for it. By changing whom he spent time with, KG was able to focus on his goals—and in the long run was also able to remain friends with his teammate. The separation between Simpson and KG caused Simpson to re-evaluate whom he needed to surround himself with.

The people you associate with will have a huge impact on who you are and how you behave. Make sure you surround yourself with the kind of people you respect and admire—those you want to emulate. Ask yourself: What type of guys are you surrounding yourself with? Whom are you hanging around at work? How about the guys you call close friends? What do they talk about when it's just you guys in the conversation? What do their actions say about who they are? Are they always pointing out the girls with the short skirts or the low-cut tops? Do they email crude jokes or inappropriate pictures? What do they do in their spare time? Do they speak highly of their wives?

I have a friend in Dallas named Victor. He is a great guy and has always appeared to have a good relationship with his wife and kids. Victor moved up the company ladder at his job—and as he did, his love of motorcycles grew. He bought a beginner Harley, and then graduated to a bigger bike each time he was promoted. He found some guys at the Harley store who were like him: young professional types who liked to ride. They would meet up from time to time on the weekends. The more he got into it, the more he rode. That meant more time spent hanging out with his *Harley bros*, as he called them.

On one Saturday afternoon, the guys had met out at the lake and cruised around. They stopped at a park and, as they sat and talked, the conversation became more and more inappropriate. Some of the guys were bashing their wives, and some were making comments about the young girls in bikinis close by. Victor told me later that he didn't think much of it at the time. You know, guys being guys.

But he found these friends were starting to get comfortable with one another—and the more comfortable they felt, the more they opened up about who they really were. On another weekend ride, they stopped at a sports bar to grab a beverage and cool off while watching a game. Victor found out that "a beverage," to these guys, was about 20 beers. The more the beer flowed, the rougher the language got. Victor left before the rest of the group and made up his mind that these were not the type of guys he wanted to associate with.

He went home and told his wife what had happened. To his surprise, she was relieved. When he asked her why she was so happy, she said that whenever he came home after hanging out with his Harley bros he was different: He was a little sharp to her and their two daughters.

"It takes you a few hours to return to your normal self," Victor's wife told him.

She had chalked it up to being a stage. She'd convinced herself that this was something that he needed—seeing as he was living in an estrogen-filled home with no other males! But now she helped Victor realize that the company he had been keeping was having a big effect on him, which he hadn't even realized.

This principle holds just as true for your wife as it does for you. It is important for her to hang out with women who will be a good influence on her. Face it, guys: There are plenty of men out there who are not great husbands. If your wife's friend is married to one of those guys, it is possible she is sharing her frustration with your wife. So make sure the number one influence in your marriage is *you*. Carve out time to discuss with your wife how you are selecting your friends and whom you're spending time with at work. Gently find out about her friends. This doesn't mean automatically dropping friends who are struggling in their marriages or who don't have their lives together. But both you and your wife need to be intentional about impacting those lives and not vice versa. Just like KG, we all have to make wise decisions about whom we are going to team up with if we want to stay on the right path.

Finally, and maybe most important, it is critical that you are aware of whom your kids are teaming up with. I live in a small town, so it is pretty easy for my wife and me. We know everybody and everybody knows us. We moved here for this very reason. It may be harder for you. My commute to work is a 20-second climb of my stairs. I take my kids to school or pick them up almost every day. All of this was by design. I go to school and have lunch with my boys regularly, although I will admit it is becoming less frequently, at their request, the older they get. I am lucky that my profession allows me to enjoy this lifestyle. My wife's schedule has similar flexibility. This may not be possible for you. I understand that. You may spend an hour or more commuting to and from work, and a responsibility to be in the office by seven or eight in the morning. You may be required to attend a lot of evening meetings. Whatever the challenges, find a way to be creative and overcome them. Being present in your kids' lives, and knowing their friends, is vitally important.

I've heard many parents, and even some psychologists, talk about giving kids their space and not intruding in their lives. I'm no psychologist but I am here to tell you that, in my humble opinion, that is a bunch of bull. You are responsible for your kids—and if they are not willing to tell you whom they are running around with, that is your first clue that you had better find out!

Also make sure you know their friends' parents. I had a friend when I was young who was a good kid but whose parents were not such great parents. Whenever I went over to his house, we were left unsupervised and, while we were both pretty well behaved, we were still kids. You can't be too careful when it comes to your kids. This might sound a little like helicopter parenting, but I can live with that label in this case. I'm not saying you need to hover over your kids at all times, but I am saying you can't be too careful about whom you trust to have responsibility for their well-being. Discuss this with your children and make sure they know that you aren't going to constantly hover over them, but that you aren't going to give them free rein either.

I mentioned earlier that Kevin Mathis found Deion Sanders to be a great mentor. Later in his career, Mathis, once the mentee, became the mentor. Kevin knew what it meant to have one of the all-time great cornerbacks help him develop as a player. The next natural step was for Kevin to take a younger player under his wing. He knew that not every player would be advised to find a mentor, so he took it upon himself to find someone he could invest in and encourage.

This mentor relationship closely resembles the discipleship relationship. It's not enough to avoid the guys who are going to lead you down the wrong path. I also recommend that you find a mature believer who will sow some wisdom into your life about how to be successful at home. On the flip side, you can learn things from being the mentor that you can't learn from being the mentee. You might feel like you are not qualified to disciple another man. That's okay. That is why you keep getting discipled while you are discipling someone else. What better way for men to become stronger and more mature in their faith than to sow into each other's lives? The Bible says, in Proverbs 27:17, "Iron sharpens iron, and one man sharpens another." A lot of men like to quote this passage, but the truth of it is that when iron is sharpening iron, there is friction and it can even be quite painful. My best friend will tell me the truth, even when it hurts. That's the type of teammate you want to surround yourself with.

When I was in junior high, a new kid moved to town and everyone liked him. When he started leading me in a direction I wasn't comfortable with, though, I backed off. The kids who *didn't* distance themselves from this boy went down a road I'm glad I didn't travel. It is the same now. If we hang out with men who do not put a high value on spending time with their kids, honoring their wives and pursuing Christ, then we can find ourselves going down a road we wouldn't choose. Be aware of who is influencing you. Tune in to your kids' friends and your wife's friends. Make sure you are being a good teammate to your family by encouraging each person to surround themselves with other good teammates.

GamePlan

- Take inventory of who is influencing you. Consider those you spend time with as well as those (authors, speakers, entertainers, and so on) whose examples or counsel you may follow from a distance. Are these individuals worthy of your admiration? Make sure you have the right teammates.

- Talk to your wife about her friends and their influence on her. Without making blanket statements about whom she should or should not spend time with, communicate any concerns.

- Talk to your kids about who is influencing them. Ask them what they like about the kids who are their closest friends. Make sure you know those children and their parents. Keep your home open to your kids' friends and be present when they are there.

- Share with your family about the important relationships in your life—how they have looked in the past and how they look now. Be honest about any poor choices you have made. Also share about how having good friends has had a positive impact on you.

- Make discipleship a part of your life and the life of your family. Ask God to connect your family with people who can serve as mentors and with those you can mentor.

26

Practice, Practice, Practice

Greg Wesley learned early in life that nothing worth having would come easy. Greg played safety for the Kansas City Chiefs after being drafted in the third round from the University of Arkansas-Pine Bluff. But his career had begun years before.

As a young kid, Greg studied great NFL players, learned the secrets to playing his position well, and worked harder than most players I know. In high school, he observed what the other players were doing and made sure he did more. He knew that if he was going to play college football, then he was going to have to be better than anybody else at his high school. If he did only the minimum required, he would end up like everybody else. Rather than just doing the minimum, Greg put in extra work when all the other players were finished, and it paid off.

Greg played safety at Arkansas-Pine Bluff, which doesn't have NFL scouts beating down the football office doors each year. But Greg knew he wanted to play on football's biggest stage, and he knew he had put in the work to earn that opportunity. After Greg's redshirt junior year, he started planning out his winter training schedule to get ready for spring ball. But just after the fall semester ended, the school's compliance department informed Greg that he was not going to have any more eligibility. He had to prepare for the NFL on short notice. Many players would have panicked and stressed out over the injustice of the situation. Greg just turned his attention to the NFL. The training was intense, but after he received his invitation to the NFL Scouting Combine in Indianapolis, Greg was rejuvenated. He knew he was going to have to perform well in Indy and he was taking no chances.

Greg did perform well in Indianapolis and his draft day stock kept shooting up. By the time the draft rolled around in April, Greg was the twenty-third pick in the third round, selected by the Kansas City Chiefs. Greg did not look at the NFL draft as the finish line, however. He saw it as the starting line. Greg did not just aspire to be in the NFL; he wanted to play in the NFL. He knew that there were 45 players who suited up on game day and only 11 that started on defense. He knew that most NFL teams had 4 or 5 safeties on the roster, but only 2 were starters and the others played primarily on special teams. Greg wanted to play. He wanted to start, and he knew it would take a lot to win the job. True to form, he was willing to do what it took to do just that. Greg was always thankful for the blessing of playing professional football, but he was never surprised that he made it. That was his plan all along, and instead of getting down every time he experienced a setback, he used the challenge as motivation and hit the practice field one more time.

Life is like sport in this regard: We don't get better through osmosis; instead we must practice to improve. Practice is tiring and tedious, but in order to win, families must train as a team in the direction they want to go together.

I like to say, "Things move at the speed of life." You graduate from college, blink, and you are married, pursuing a career and having your first child. You blink again and your child is going into high school and looking at colleges. Maybe you are one of those guys who blinked a third time, and now you are spending time with your grandchildren! Because things move so fast, you have to make sure one season doesn't turn into a whole career without your ever taking the time to do the things you want to do with your team.

I had an aha moment in 2010. I was coming down the stairs from my home office; when I was about halfway down, I looked into the kitchen, where my wife and boys were hanging out. The boys were sitting down, about to eat dinner, and my wife was putting their plates together. They were all laughing and having a great time. It was one of those rare moments when my boys, then 9 and

11, weren't pounding on each other, and I thought, *Does God know what He's doing, giving me responsibility for these three human beings?* I have never felt as incapable or unqualified to lead my family as I did at that moment. Have you ever felt that way? There are times when everything is rocking along, smooth as can be, and I don't even think twice about it. But when I look head-on at the enormous responsibility I have taken on, it can be overwhelming. I made a vow in that moment that I would not just play the game. I would approach being a dad and a husband with the same tenacity that Greg Wesley applied to making it to the NFL.

David wasn't picking up a sling for the first time when he squared off against Goliath. He had spent hours upon hours in the nasty sheep pen, slinging rocks at posts and trees. He then spent many days defending the sheep from lions and bears. He had practiced and practiced and practiced. So when he came down from the hillside, into the valley, and saw the Israelites squared off against the Philistines, he didn't hesitate to look Goliath in the eye and say, "Who are you to come against the children of the most high God?" He knew that God had prepared him for that exact moment. I call that something inside of David "a little bit of crazy," and I think God gave all men the same thing. We need it to accomplish everything He has given us to do. We have to juggle a lot, manage a lot and be willing to literally lay down our lives for our families. God knew all of this and He designed us to be able to handle it. My best friend, Michael Chenoweth, says of things he likes a lot, "That's greatness." That is my goal as the leader of my home: I want to embody greatness. When I had my epiphany, I decided good wasn't good enough when it comes to my family. I have to strive for greatness. David knew a good shot wouldn't put the giant down. He knew he needed greatness with his sling and he had practiced enough to have greatness.

One of the first lessons I learned after becoming a sports agent is that most people hold an unrealistic view of the lives of professional athletes. Contrary to popular belief, NFL players do not practice for a few hours a few days a week, play on Sundays, and party through every other waking moment. In order to achieve success, a player must pledge allegiance to the old sports cliché: *practice, practice, practice.*

Most NFL players start their days at 6 A.M. That is when they have to be in for treatment for the injuries they sustained during the game on Sunday. Then at 7:30 they start having meetings. There is usually a team meeting first, followed by a position meeting where they review the tape from the previous week. After a short break, they have a walkthrough of the practice they will participate in later that afternoon. After the walkthrough, they have another position meeting to review the game plan for the week's opponent, followed by lunch. After lunch, players have offense and defense meetings, followed by practice. After practice, they have another position meeting, where they watch the tape of the practice they just finished. This is followed by special teams meetings and more treatment. At 6 P.M. they head home.

Everybody likes to play the game. The game is the fun part. The game is exciting and energizing. What we don't like to do is practice. Practice is boring, tedious and tiring. However, most of us like to win—and in order to win, we need to be good at the details. That takes practice.

Vince Lombardi was known for starting the first practice of every new season by holding up a football and saying, "Men, this is a football . . ." His point was that you have to start with the fundamentals. He was also quoted as saying, "Winning is not a sometime thing, it is an all the time thing. You don't do things right once in a while. . . you do them right all the time."[1] Lombardi was a stickler for tending to the details, and that requires practice.

My commitment to be a great leader for my family was conceived in that moment on my staircase, as I watched the most incredible gift God has ever given me: my family. I vowed that I would not let the speed of life steal my family from me. I had been doing the big things fairly well. I was blessed to have led both of my boys to a saving knowledge of Christ. My wife and I had been through a debilitating illness together, we have an unbelievable marriage, and I have a blessed business. But the details—the little things that take a home from good to great—were missing.

Chuck Knoll was one of the most successful coaches in the NFL. My friend Tony Dungy recalls that when he was a rookie and was playing for Coach Knoll, the great coach told him, "Champions are not champions because they do anything extraordinary but because they do the ordinary things better than anyone else." That's a great message to remember as you lead your home. Don't settle for good or even *really* good. I encourage you to strive for greatness—for doing the ordinary things of life as excellently as you possibly can.

Those teams, individuals and families that understand achieving greatness know it will require that they practice, practice, practice.

GamePlan

- Make a commitment to follow through with the Game Plans provided in each chapter—they will only help if you practice them on a regular basis.

- Put principles into practice, but don't feel like you have to do everything at once—or even everything at all. Talk things over with your wife and see what makes the most sense for your family at this stage of your lives. Then tackle these Game Plans one at a time. If you are a single dad, don't despair. Do what you can when you can.

- Be intentional about the things you want to instill in your children. Don't get swept away by the speed of life. Take time, on your own and with your wife, to assess how things are going and to plan your next steps.

Note

1. "Famous Quotes by Vince Lombardi," Vince Lombardi (Family of Vince Lombardi: Luminary Group LLC, 2010). vincelombardi.com/quotes.html (accessed March 2014).

27

Always Move Forward

There is only one acceptable direction for an offense to move in football: forward. If the ball is not advancing, the offense is not doing their job. But sometimes forward progression means trying something that doesn't work, backing up, and then employing a new or creative tactic.

Ron Rivers was one of the first good players I worked with, and our relationship had an interesting beginning. I recruited Ron, but when it came time to make a decision, he went with a more experienced agent. It was hard to blame him, but I wanted to work with this hard-running tailback from Fresno State in a big way. He'd played in the Senior Bowl and the East-West Shrine game, and I'd never represented a player who had played in an All-Star game. Ron had played well in both games, and he had a decent Combine, but on draft day he didn't hear his name called.

Some of the perks of signing with a bigger agent at the time were per diem payments for living expenses and assistance with getting a new car prior to the draft. Among other drawbacks, that practice had the player starting off in a financial hole. Although I advised against the car, against changing his lifestyle prior to the draft, and against borrowing money against his NFL contract, Ron ultimately made these choices. Before you judge Ron, you should know that most players were offered such perks and most players accepted them.

After his disappointing draft day experience, Ron did some soul searching. His conclusion was that he needed better advice from someone he could count on to give it to him straight. He fired his previous agent and hired me. He signed with the San Diego Chargers as a free agent. Ron had a good camp and a nice preseason. It appeared he was going to have a great chance to make the active roster. He was moving forward. The cuts came and Ron made the final cut. He was still moving forward. But the day after the final cuts, the Indianapolis Colts released a big back with great blocking skills named Rodney Culver. In an effort to find a guy who might be better suited to pick up the blitz on third down, the Chargers cut Ron and signed Culver. Now Ron was going backward. Yet, a few weeks later, he was signed to the Detroit Lions practice squad. He was going forward again.

Ron ended up playing seven seasons in the NFL, six of which were with the Lions. While in Detroit, Ron was the backup to one of the NFL's all-time great running backs, Barry Sanders. The interesting thing is the way Ron's career mirrored Sanders' running style. Sanders was known to shoot out of the backfield like he was fired from a cannon, make a cut sideways at the same speed he had been moving forward, and then go backward 10 yards to find a hole that would allow him to go the distance. He would have a higher than average number of negative yardage runs every year, but he was always found at the top of the league in total yards rushing. Similarly, Ron would get a nominal amount of carries every year but was consistently named the Lions' Special Teams Player of the Year. Still, he would long for more opportunities to run the football. When Sanders surprised everybody and abruptly retired after the 1998 season, Ron got his chance to be the featured back. He was no longer going sideways. He made the most of the opportunity until a leg injury cut his season short. Ron had gone one step forward and two steps back, then three steps forward and another step back—just like Sanders' running style.

Despite the various setbacks he faced, Ron didn't look back and he didn't stay in the past. Ultimately, like Sanders, his forward momentum won the day. Similarly, in life, we cannot spend our time looking back and living in the past. Too many parents romanticize the good ol' days, when their responsibilities were fewer and life seemed simpler. But such a view of the past is neither realistic nor helpful. Rather, we need to release the past and trust God in the present. The Bible says, "Be still, and know that I am God" (Ps. 46:10). The *New American Standard Bible* version says, "Cease striving . . ." I like to say, "Be chill, and let God be God." He doesn't need our skills to move us forward. He just wants us to be willing and available. Living in the past and fearing the future are like moving sideways and backward without ever finding the hole and sprinting the 50 yards to the end zone. Just like the guy who was the starting quarterback in high school but hasn't done anything since, we can be tempted to lean on our past achievements. In our careers, this can look like having some initial success and creating great expectations at a company, only to see things level off and the promotions that came so quickly early on no longer come.

It can be hard to release the *good* in our past, and it can also be hard to release the *bad*—specifically, the wrongs committed against us by others. This can be toxic to the survival of one's family. Nothing can destroy relationships—inside a family and out—like bitterness. Perhaps just the mention of bitter people conjures up the mental image of at least one person you know. Bitterness is caused by unforgiveness. You have probably heard the saying that refusing to forgive someone is like drinking poison and expecting *someone else* to die from it! You can't move forward in your life if you continue to nurse the wrongs committed against you.

A friend shared a story with me the other day about a situation that had happened to him. The perpetrator was a former neighbor who was at the time a great friend. The situation had caused the friendship to fracture and prompted my friend to move. He ranted a little and then confidently stated, "But I have forgiven him." I almost laughed out loud. I asked him why, if he had forgiven his former friend, he went on about the story for so long. He stopped and carefully considered my question; then he concluded, "Maybe I have some more forgiving to do."

I had a client who was a backup linebacker and a great special teams player. His team was playing in Kansas City toward the end of the 2008 season and they were in contention for the division championship. Late in the game, they were lined up in punt formation deep in their own end of the field, clinging to a three-point lead, with the clock working to their advantage. They had a four-time all-pro punter, and the Chiefs had lost their starting QB on the previous series. The feeling was that if this team could get a decent punt off and limit the return, it would be an uphill battle for the Chiefs to win the game.

My client was on the far left side of the formation. Kansas City knew their best opportunity to pull out the victory was to block the punt. They shifted several players to the far side, overloading the area where my client was lined up. The ball was snapped and the Chiefs ran a quick stunt, freezing my client's teammate, and, you guessed it, the punt was blocked. A Chiefs player scooped up the ball and scampered into the end zone for a touchdown. The extra point made it a four-point lead with 24 seconds left. To make matters worse, the all-pro punter was injured on the play.

I still remember the moment like it was yesterday. I was at another client's game and was watching on TV in the club level of a stadium thousands of miles away. I stood up, repeating "No, no, no, no," over and over as the play unfolded. Watching the replay, it looked like my client did the right thing—sliding to his left to pick up the outside man, who was looping around his teammate. The player next to my client appeared to have responsibility for the next closest outside rusher but instead took the man directly in front of him, leaving a man free to have a clean shot at the punter. The intended effect was accomplished: There was confusion over who would take whom.

I sent my client a text and asked him to give me a call when he could. We caught up later that evening. I asked what the coaches had said about that play, expecting that they would have put the blame on the other guy.

My client, not being a man of many words, said, "Coach told me it was on me."

"Are you kidding me?" I exclaimed.

My client went on to tell me that the punter had suffered a torn ACL.

I asked him if there was something I didn't see, and he replied, "No, I did what I was coached to do in the situation."

He didn't harp on it, but it was obvious: Being blamed for a season-ending loss and the injury of a teammate was grating on him. The following off-season was the worst of his career. It just seemed like he never recovered from being blamed for the play. When training camp started, he was not the player he had been in the past. I thought that maybe he'd lost his confidence, so I constantly tried to build him up. He ended up getting cut that year. When he called to tell me, he mentioned being blamed for the blocked punt that led to the season-ending loss *and* for getting the punter hurt. He couldn't let it go and move forward, and that ended up costing him his career. He had a couple of opportunities with other teams, but he had the same results. He never played in an NFL game again.

I love the song "Redeemed" by Big Daddy Weave. One line goes like this:

> Then You look at this prisoner and say to me, "Son, Stop fighting a fight that's already been won."[1]

That's what living in the past is like: living as a prisoner, fighting a fight that's already been won. If you want to produce a winning family, learn to dream about the future and stop living in the past.

GamePlan

- Identify past bitterness and let it go. If you need to, seek out a trusted friend or a professional counselor to help you address old wounds that need to be healed.

- Don't cling to past successes. Identify new goals and determine to strive toward them.

- Huddle up with your family and discuss why it is so important to live in the moment, rather than leaning on your past successes or failing to move beyond wrongs that were committed against you. Encourage family members to acknowledge areas where they are stuck in the past, and commit to moving forward together.

Note
1. Mike Weaver and Benji Cowart, "Redeemed," *Big Daddy Weave: Love Come to Life* (Word Records, 2012).

28

Commit, Don't Quit

After a successful college career playing wide receiver for the University of South Florida, Carlton Mitchell was drafted by the Cleveland Browns in 2010. Not only had Carlton *not* had NFL dreams as a young child, but also he'd never even played football until the tenth grade! He'd played soccer and baseball, and had been involved in boxing, but not football.

It wasn't until his junior year in high school that Carlton ever thought about playing in college. It was then that he made a commitment to himself, and to his mother, that he was going to play college football. Keeping that commitment wasn't easy, but Carlton never backed down. He just kept working.

Carlton led the team in receptions and receiving touchdowns as a freshman at South Florida. The summer between his freshman and sophomore years, he made another commitment: He was going to play in the NFL. Carlton developed a reputation for being one of the hardest workers on the team. He knew that playing in the NFL was not going to just happen, so he put in the work required to make it happen. His commitment included waking up early during the summer to get his workouts in. It meant he had to modify his diet to properly fuel his body, and he had to get extra sleep to perform at peak efficiency. He was determined to be the best he could be. After successful sophomore and junior campaigns, Carlton made the jump to the NFL. His commitment had paid off.

In a world where it is commonplace for kids to grow up without a father figure in their lives—as Carlton did—many children grow up without an understanding of what commitment means.

But Carlton's mom, Angela, is a strong woman who made sure her son knew what commitment meant. She worked hard to provide for Carlton and his sister, and she showed them what commitment looked like. Angela was working as an operating room anesthesia nurse when a friend introduced her to professional light heavyweight boxer Antonio Tarver. Tarver was looking for a "cut man"—the assistant who deals with cuts sustained by a boxer during a fight—and he hired Angela. So she added the second job. Carlton saw firsthand the commitment it took for Tarver to win the light heavyweight title. Today, Carlton credits his mother and Tarver as key contributors to his ability to commit, both professionally and personally.

Without complete commitment, it is easy to quit. Most every spouse, in the darkest nights and roughest seasons, considers packing a bag and leaving. This is why complete commitment—no matter how exhausting or painful it becomes—is required to make a marriage succeed. Similarly, when your kids are behaving poorly—as if they've never been taught anything about the real world or how life works—you must remain committed to shaping their lives with love and discipline.

One rule every man should establish in his marriage is, "Don't ever use the *D* word" (divorce). I have a friend, Jenson, who lives in a different city, but we communicate regularly. He is a hardworking man with three kids. Several years ago, he confided in me that he and his wife were not getting along. His story is similar to many. You probably know a couple with similar struggles. Jenson travels for his job. His wife, Sara, works taking care of the kids and the home.

"Being away four days a week is hard," Jenson confided to me in private. "I feel separated from the daily happenings in my family's lives—and when I get back in town, it's as if it's too hard for them to catch me up, so I feel left out and they feel I'm not involved." He added, "Sara feels I don't do enough, but she doesn't mind putting the paycheck in the bank and taking advantage of all the perks that go with it."

Jenson went on to share that he and Sara were fighting all the time, over silly stuff, each weekend when he was home—to the point that he couldn't wait to get back on the road. He'd even been considering leaving on Sunday evenings instead of Monday mornings. Jenson told me about a big fight they'd had the night before. The stress had been piling up and the intimacy had fallen off to . . . nothing. After dinner, Jenson went out to the garage to tinker around while Sara cleaned the kitchen. The kids went off to friends' houses and other activities. Jenson came back inside and told his wife they should take advantage of the alone time. Sara responded, "If you think you can just come waltzing back in town and jump in the sack with me like I'm some kind of hooker or something, you have another thing coming." Not having been in the middle of all that had gone down in their home, it was easy for me to hear the desperation on both sides of their difficult situation. But in the heat of the moment, feeling attacked and hurt, Jenson told his wife that if she kept that attitude up she would be looking for a divorce lawyer in no time.

I told Jenson he needed to apologize to Sara for even *mentioning* divorce, and to commit together with his bride that divorce would never be put on the table ever again. He needed to commit, again, to his wife and to their marriage.

Jenson did not take my advice.

He kept bringing the subject up and, after he'd broken the ice with it, Sara joined in. Jenson told me that things would be great one weekend and terrible the next. He would get random texts from Sara during the week, accusing him of having a mistress on the road, which he assured me was the furthest thing from his mind. But by bringing up the possibility of divorce, he'd broken trust. Sara did not trust him anymore, because although he'd made a vow at their wedding, he'd now verbalized that he was willing to break that vow. It was like lighting a fuse that would eventually lead to the explosion of their marriage. And that's exactly what happened.

Once Jenson let Sara know that he would be willing to break his vow, the ability to restore their marriage was gone. Without repentance and forgiveness, no amount of counseling or therapy or even "trying to work on it" could restore the trust. Jenson was the leader of his home. It was his responsibility to humble himself and ask Sara to forgive him, vowing never to threaten divorce again. Honestly, he'd have been better off if he had told her he'd die miserable with her before he would even *consider* divorce.

Just as Carlton's commitment to being the best football player he could be was visible in his stellar work habits, so too you teach your kids what real commitment is all about by demonstrating it. Our society has created a microwave mindset. Everybody wants what they want *right now*. If something takes time and hard work to attain, many people would just as soon move on to the *next* thing. Commitment as a short-term venture isn't commitment at all. But that's how so many people view it in our culture. Commitment is a long-term endeavor and requires great amounts of perseverance.

I have always loved music. I've had a desire to learn how to play guitar since I was a kid. The thing is, I never owned a guitar and I never took a lesson. I wasn't committed to learning how to play guitar; I just liked the idea of being able to play. Ten years ago, I made a commitment to learn how to play guitar. I bought a guitar and started taking lessons. I didn't just buy a starter guitar. I bought an expensive Taylor guitar. Jeff, the intern in our youth ministry at church, was an awesome guitarist and he agreed to give me lessons. I will admit, I was not a natural. But I stuck with it and Jeff was patient. Then he graduated from seminary and took a job three states away. I practiced on my own, but without a teacher I found it hard to keep up with it. When I moved into my new house, with a new office, I bought a stand and displayed my Taylor in my office. I look at it every day and sometimes even pick it up and play the three chords I know. I will learn how to play it one day. I'm committed. I could probably sell the guitar for close to what I paid for it, but I'm not giving up on the dream.

My boys have learned that when you agree to do something, you do it. Once we commit to something in our family, there is no backing out or changing our minds. Sometimes, it's true, teaching that lesson becomes a burden on Layne and me! For example, Eli decided at six years old that he was going to play tee ball. Although we're not a baseball family, Eli wanted to play. So we signed him up and bought him a glove. Three practices in, and prior to playing a single game, Eli announced that he was retiring from tee ball.

Being completely candid, everything within me wanted to find a reason to say okay! Watching tee ball is *excruciating*. The coach puts the ball on the tee; the kid takes a big long swing and hits the tee right in the middle; and the ball falls to the ground. The coach puts the ball back on the tee and the whole scene is repeated. It took some kids *10 tries* to actually hit the ball. Eli would sit in the infield playing with the sand, and I wanted to join him. But we told him that because he had committed to the team, he had to finish the season. I sat through eight tee ball games, praying the whole time that Eli would never want to play again.

I see parents sign their kids up for two and three sports in the same season. They can't commit to any of them completely, so every team is dealing with players who have a half-way commitment. It teaches kids to overcommit and under-deliver and sets a bad precedent. Total commitment is a learned behavior. Similarly, a lack of commitment is also a learned behavior

My kids know several things for certain: Their mom and dad will be married (to each other!) until one or both of us dies. They know that no matter what they do, Layne and I will love them and be there for them. They know that the Creator of the universe loves them and is there for them. He has a plan for them and they can trust that. Each boy also knows that his brother will always love him, even though he treats him like a jerk half the time. My wife knows that I love her and am committed to her, not based on her behavior or actions but based on my word. I know that she has the same commitment to me. Without commitment, a winning family is not possible. *With* commitment, a winning family is inevitable.

GamePlan

- To teach your kids commitment, you may have to learn how to commit yourself. If it wasn't modeled for you earlier in your life, learn what it means and get with a mentor now to help you. Ask your mentor and/or your family members to hold you accountable to any commitments you make.

- Communicate your commitment to your wife and to your kids by your words and your actions. Do you view quitting like it's no big deal? Keep a close eye on your vocabulary—never, ever, ever use the *D* word.

- Teach your kids to honor their commitments. Help them think about how adding a new activity will affect their schedule, and if they can truly commit to it. If they do, be ready to support them in keeping the commitment.

29

Learn How to Win

In November 2007, I was driving away from Baylor's Floyd Casey Stadium with my father-in-law, former Baylor football coach Grant Teaff. Baylor had just suffered its eighth loss in a row, a 45-14 tail kicking, to finish the season with a 3-9 record. It was the Bears' twelfth losing season in a row.

As we inched along in traffic, I felt Coach Teaff's dejection. He had spent 21 years building Baylor football into a respectable program, achieving far more than anyone would have guessed possible. Now that program was crumbling before his eyes.

"The hardest part," he explained, "is that the team is so used to losing. They have to learn how to win again."

Any coach who has ever taken on rebuilding a program will tell you that a losing mentality is a huge obstacle. Losing is like a disease you can't get out of your system. Just when you think you are all clear, it rears its ugly head again, infiltrating every aspect of your program. Coach Teaff knew this firsthand, from facing down the challenge when he'd arrived in Waco charged with the task of bringing the lowly Bears back from the Southwest Conference cellar. Learning how to win again requires a good system, key individuals and the right attitude. Coach Teaff brought a system. He had key individuals in the form of coaches and the players he would recruit. And he brought an attitude of expectation. Expectation isn't just about convincing everyone that they're winners. The expectation to win involves both desire and the commitment to putting in the work.

Art Briles came to Baylor in 2008 to bring the Bears back, once again, from the conference cellar. He brought an offensive system that was known for putting up gaudy numbers. He brought a coaching staff that knew the system and was committed to it. He also brought one of the top recruits in the country, a QB named Robert Griffin III. But equally important, his system included an attitude, and that attitude included a component of perseverance.

The ship would require a slow and steady turn. The Bears went 4-8 during each of their first two seasons under Briles. Two four-victory seasons may not seem like success to many, but learning how to win requires a few wins! The victories, few though they may be, need to be celebrated. The taste of victory has to be savored and appreciated so that players want more of it.

There is a saying in the South that people use when somebody goes after something with perseverance. They say that person went after it "like a dog on a bone." A dog will get a taste for the bone, and he'll pick up the scent, and he won't stop until he has it. Celebrating victories is what gives players a taste for winning so that they have to have it. Briles's third year brought seven victories and Baylor's first bowl game in 15 years. Currently the Bears are ranked twelfth in the nation and have the number one offense in the nation.

Another coach who has discovered a formula for turning programs around is Brian Kelly. Kelly was a successful coach at Grand Valley State before departing to Central Michigan, where the Chippewas had not won more than four games in any of the previous four seasons. In his third season at Central Michigan, Kelly won the Mid-Atlantic Conference and the Motor City Bowl. From Central Michigan, Kelly was hired to take over the Cincinnati Bearcats. He had immediate success, including bowl games in every season and two conference championships. He has since taken over at the University of Notre Dame, a storied program that had suffered from underperformance for several years in a row. Kelly brought a system, key individuals and an attitude to Notre Dame, and in his third season he took the Fighting Irish to the National Championship game. His all-time head coaching record is an impressive 203-70-2.

The same principles apply in your home. When you've generated consistent losses—fights with the children, miscommunication with your spouse, dysfunctional family dynamics—it is very easy to forget how to create wins. Losing is contagious. But so is winning. Married life and parenting will not always be a smooth road, and sometimes the difficulties make family members want to run away from home—even as adults! But don't give up; to win big in the long run, a family must first focus on generating small but consistent wins every day—like simple acts of kindness, siblings working things out themselves without coming to blows, or spouses having a disagreement and coming to a workable conclusion instead of letting it escalate into something bigger. Doing this takes a system, key individuals and the right attitude. You are the leader, so bringing these components together is your responsibility. As the head coach, you get to choose your system.

My system involves creating a team environment. We are all on the same team. We get to communicate our displeasure with our teammates, but only in a constructive, non-violent way. We accept that none of us is perfect, so when a teammate lets another one down, we give that person the grace we want when we are the one letting someone down. Sounds easy, right? It isn't. It takes time, and it can be like turning a big ship. Change happens gradually.

A corollary to the constructive criticism principle is that although someone on the team can criticize the team, outsiders can't. We stick up for one another. Anyone who attacks my teammate is attacking me. Another component of my system is that we have goals. We determine the goals together, and then we divide and conquer. If the goal is to have the yard mowed, the laundry done and the house picked up so we can go do something fun as a family, we all pitch in so the work gets done and we can enjoy the fun together. Again, this is not easy. Usually Layne and I are the ones who want the work done, while the boys just want to do something fun. But if we take the teamwork approach, we generally find that the results are better.

The key individuals in this case aren't high-paid or widely touted recruits you can go after. They're the ones you are stuck with! I'm not saying this in a derogatory way. I just mean that you have your team already. You can't recruit a new player. You get to develop the players you have, and you get to coach your assistant head coach—your wife. All great coaches coach their coaches.

We just hired a new head football coach/athletic director at our high school here in Salado. His name is Brent Graham and he is awesome. He took over a great situation and took it to an even greater level of excellence. Coach Graham evaluated his team and saw that he had good coaches who he knew could be great. He is investing in his key individuals. He didn't stop with the high school coaches. He is also coaching the junior high coaches. One of the first things a great coach does when coaching his coaches is to get their feedback on what the state of the program is and their ideas about what can be done better. This is a good thing to do with your wife. If you impose your ideas on her without getting her feedback, you will have other issues. Conversely, if you have a strong-willed wife, and you allow her to take the lead, you are putting your team in a state of imbalance that God did not intend for your family. On a football team, especially in college, the strength and conditioning coach spends more time with the players than anybody else, so he is critical to the success of the team. He has a finger on the pulse of the team like no other member of the coaching staff. But the strength and conditioning coach is not the head coach and can't be given those duties.

The other key individuals are your kids. As you develop leadership qualities in your kids, and figure out their individual strengths and abilities, you can put them in the right positions to help the team win. Each of us receives unique gifts from God. Just as you wouldn't put a defensive tackle at quarterback, because he does not have those abilities, so too you don't want to put a child in the wrong position. Remember what we discussed before about making sure each team member is playing to his or her strengths—for their sakes as well as for the sake of the team as a whole. The development of players is what makes some teams consistently better than others. You are responsible for the program to develop your wife and kids.

Last, but certainly not least, my system is heavy on a positive attitude. Learning to win requires believing that you can. It is about creating an atmosphere conducive to a positive attitude. It's not about the eight losses in the season; it's about focusing on the four victories. It's okay to talk about how you felt about the losses, but only as motivation to not have any more. In my system, we savor the victories. We celebrate them and talk about how we got there.

In the fifth grade, Eli just wanted to get by. He didn't seem to care about learning or about what kind of grades he made in math. I was the same way as a kid, so I understood. He doesn't like math. That's fine, but he has to take it—and he was not even halfway through his school years at this point. I kept telling him he didn't have to *like* it but he needed to *care*. When he was in sixth grade, I picked him up from school one day and he was in a *terrible* mood. He threw his backpack and lunchbox into the car and slammed the door. I questioned him and he said he had made a bad grade on a math test. You know what? We celebrated that victory. Not the bad grade—we celebrated the fact that he cared. I had asked him to care and he did. Caring is a positive.

A loss or a setback is a coaching point—an opportunity to learn what not to do so that we can get back to the victories. My system stays away from absolutes such as "he always does that" or "you never let me . . ." Avoiding those absolutes also applies to us parents. I have to watch saying things like, "You never pick up your room" or "You always leave your dirty socks in the living room." Absolutes program people to actually do what you don't want them to do. They *program* a bad attitude. It is better to say, "I can't remember the last time I came in your room and there wasn't a wet towel on the floor. Can you remind me?" My son might reply, "I hung it up yesterday," and I say, "All right, I'm sorry I missed that one. High five." Sounds goofy, but he doesn't walk away feeling beat up. He walks away thinking, *I like high fives better than getting yelled at*, and is motivated to hang up his towel. It is all about the attitude I want and the atmosphere I create to obtain that attitude.

You get to develop your own system. The most important factor is to have one. Don't just hope and pray that your family will become the people you want them to be. You probably have desired behaviors and character traits you want to see exhibited in your family. Be intentional. Give your family members some direction. Losses pile up and usually lead to more losses. Ask any coach. Losing momentum moves fast and easy. Learn how to win and it becomes a driving force.

GamePlan

- Identify what a win looks like for your family. Sometimes a win is simply the opposite of the losses you are currently experiencing, so start there. Identify milestones you can celebrate along the way to the win you desire.

- Put your system in place. What fundamental principles will strengthen your functioning as a family?

- Open communication with your key individuals. Do you know what your children's gifts, strengths and interests are? How about your wife's? Once you know this, put your players in the positions they are designed for and help your players develop their skills and grow into new roles.

- Assume responsibility for the team's attitude. Define the attitude you want and work to create an atmosphere conducive to the desired attitude. Model the attitude you want to see in your team.

30

Create a Champion-Level Legacy

I grew up in Richardson, Texas, a suburb of Dallas, and I quickly became a fan of the Dallas Cowboys. My dad bought season tickets and we went to every home game until I was well out of college. One of my earliest childhood memories is of going to the Cotton Bowl one blustery fall afternoon to watch my beloved Cowboys take on the Minnesota Vikings. It was a battle between superstar quarterbacks Don Meredith and Fran Tarkenton.

I remember staring at a stoic figure on the Dallas sideline in a funny-looking hat. Of course, it was legendary head coach Tom Landry. He always looked so serious. The Cowboys were coming off of a 52-7 drubbing of Landry's former team, the New York Giants, for which he played and was an assistant coach. I asked my dad how Landry could stand to beat his team so bad, and my dad explained that the *Cowboys* were his team now. Little did my dad know, at the time, just how right he would prove to be. Landry's vision for the Cowboys was not just to win games but also to create a champion-level legacy. He did both.

Coach Landry was from Mission, Texas, and attended the University of Texas. He served in the United States Army Air Corps during World War II. He was drafted by the New York Giants and played six seasons for the team. During the last two, he was also the defensive coordinator. He was committed to his faith and was never swayed by the glitz of New York or Dallas. Coach Landry and his wife, Alicia, were close friends of Coach Teaff and my mother-in-law, Donell. One of the coolest moments in my life was talking to Coach and Alicia when they attended my wedding to Layne.

Coach Landry retired after the 1988 season, when Jerry Jones bought the team. He went to be with the Lord in February 2000, after a brief battle with cancer. In October 2001, Jerry Jones unveiled a 20-foot statue of the championship coach.

When the statue was presented during the halftime of a game, Alicia Landry was asked what she thought of the enormous statue.

"I remember him being bigger," she said as she stared up at her husband's towering likeness.

Watching, I thought, *That's what I want my family to say about me when I'm gone!*

I also realized that I'm contributing to their memory of me right now. Every Saturday, I choose to coach one of the boys' teams; instead of going on the road to watch a potential client play, I am putting a deposit in the memory bank of my sons. I have opportunities to attend all sorts of games and events. I pass on most of these invitations so that I can be at home with my wife. I want her to understand that our relationship is the most important one in my life. I want my boys to remember me being present and sowing into their lives.

I have a friend in the agent business who, when we met, was moving and shaking. He was living in Colorado while his family was living in Georgia. He had some investors who had partnered with him to build a sports representation and marketing business. My friend is sharp, and he was well on his way to making a name for himself and his partners.

I ran into him at an all-star game one year and he looked tired. I spent some time with him and asked how he was doing. He talked for a good while about the new clients his agency had signed, the other sports they were getting into, and the growth of the marketing side of their business. He spoke of expansion and possibly moving to a more significant city.

I stopped him and asked how *he* was doing. After a little pause, as though he had to check in with himself, he answered that he was pretty tired and that he missed his family. He admitted that living in two places and missing his kids' events was hard. My friend is a committed follower of Christ, and I could tell my question had struck a chord with him. I was pretty blunt and told him I thought he was missing the mark.

A little less than a year later, we met up again; this time we were at the NFL Scouting Combine in Indianapolis. My friend looked different. He had a spring in his step and looked like a million bucks. I'd heard through the agent grapevine that his company had restructured and that some changes were on the horizon. I asked him how he was and this time he told me about *himself*. He explained that our previous talk had opened his eyes to the fact that he was chasing the wind. He sold his interest in the company to his partners and was living in Georgia full-time now. He was going to his kids' events and sleeping in his own bed almost every night. He was still representing players and was actually able to be more involved with his clients because he wasn't doing all the extraneous stuff he'd been doing before. My friend is well on his way to having his family say, "I remember him being bigger."

The Bible tells us:

> Behold, children are a heritage from the LORD, the fruit of the womb a reward. Like arrows in the hand of a warrior are the children of one's youth. Blessed is the man who fills his quiver with them (Ps. 127:3-5).

Raising our children is our greatest responsibility. So often men will emphasize *providing* for our families, which isn't a bad thing. It is part of our responsibility. It is the definition of *provision* that gets men off-track sometimes. Is provision a roof over everyone's heads, food on the table and clothes on everyone's backs, or is it the biggest house in the neighborhood, steaks every night and the latest designer jeans?

I am not against economic gain or God's children being blessed. I expect it. Why shouldn't God's children be the ones with overflowing barns and vats that can't contain the blessing? That's what the Word of God tells us He has for us (see Prov. 3:9-10). We have been adopted into the family of the most-high God. We should work hard and be innovative. Those who have a full storehouse have the ability to bless others.

The rub comes when the legacy of our storehouse overshadows the legacy of our children. I used to say I wanted my kids to have it better than I had it. Really?! What's that all about? I now believe I was suffering from pride in the area of my finances. It wasn't about my children. It was about *me*; it was about having my children think more highly of me because of my success. That is not the legacy I want to leave.

My older son, Jake, is about to turn 14. He is in that interesting stage where he's not yet a man but isn't a boy anymore either. For instance, he's started thinking about the type of car he wants to drive when he turns 16. He's also starting to notice more than he has ever noticed before. He can spot inconsistencies in an adult's behavior, while even a year ago he either didn't notice or didn't care. He keeps me on my toes, that's for sure!

Jake asked me the other day if I always wanted to be a sports agent. I told him that I had wanted to be a professional athlete up until my junior year in college. He then wanted to know if I was disappointed I was never a professional athlete—a pointed question from a teenage boy. I could look him in the eyes and say no. I was honest with him and shared that there was a time, when I first saw that it wasn't going to happen for me, that I was a little frustrated by the fact. But now I know I am doing what God has called me to do.

His next observation was amazing: He noted that I had worked hard to make it in my business and that he knew my company was important to me, but he said that he believed that if God called me to sell the business, or even just shut it down, I would—and that I would do it joyfully. He also shared that he knew that no matter how important my business was, God and family came first for me. I believe that assurance is of more value than any material possessions I could ever provide for him.

When you lead a champion-level life, and leave a champion-level legacy, your legacy will loom large—just like Tom Landry's did. He affected a lot of people in a positive way, but none more than his family. As parents, we need to honor this truth. Our children will *be* our legacies long after we've left the earth. Are you taking note of and evaluating what kind of legacy you are leaving? Will your children remember you as an absent figure who was rarely available, or as a loving and present parent? Will they remember the great lessons of faith and values you taught and embodied? I encourage you to take seriously your role as a spouse and parent, and to begin building a champion-level legacy that will loom large after you cross from this world into the next.

GamePlan

- Take inventory of the current state of your legacy. If things continue as they are, how are your children likely to remember you? What will they most likely pass on to their kids?

- If need be, create a plan for turning things around. Or create a plan to take where you are headed to the next level. Think about people who loom larger than life in your own memory. What did those people do to have that kind of legacy?

- Be intentional about your actions and the long-term value lessons you are leaving your family. Do not leave your legacy to chance; make the choice to be fully present with and invested in your family.

Appendix A

Bonus Ideas

Quality Time

One of the biggest issues facing the American family is the lack of quality family time. We addressed it a little in chapter 11, "Control the Pace," but it deserves more. The older you get, the faster life goes. It seems like it should be the other way around but it isn't. I shared the story of my aha moment: I had barely taken a breath, and Jake and Eli were about to be teenagers. Now I'm staring high school and college right in the eye.

We recently went to homecoming at Layne's alma mater, Baylor University. We met up with some of her friends. These were the same people we used to run around with, until they started having kids and cramping our style. Their kids are in college now!

The point is: Take advantage of the time you have with your family. None of us knows the amount of time we have on this planet, so make the most of it. *Carpe diem!* Seize the day! Spend time with your wife. I highly recommend checking out the book *Date Your Wife*, by Justin Buzzard. The 100 creative ideas about how to date your wife in Appendix 1 are worth the cost of the book alone. Some of the ideas might surprise or even shock you, but you will like them and your wife will *love* them.

Find some fun things to do with your kids. Not long ago, Layne and I took the boys to Austin. We played putt-putt golf, and then we went swimming at Barton Springs. The water was freezing and the people were interesting. We didn't take any of the boys' friends; it was just family. We had a great time doing something new together and making it an adventure. You can do something totally different. Every family is unique, so what is fun for us might not appeal to you and your family. Just find something new and fun for you. One year we went to Colorado and spent a few days in the mountains. We went zip-lining and white water rafting. We had never done it before and it was awesome.

You don't have to travel, though, to enjoy your family. Here are some ideas to help you add quality time into your family dynamic:

1. Make date night with your wife the most important event of the week.
2. Take each child out, individually, for a fun time. Spend some time doing something that child enjoys.
3. Go bowling together.
4. Find a great hole-in-the-wall restaurant in a small city close to your hometown and make it a family outing.
5. Make some sandwiches, fill a cooler full of bottled waters, and hand them out to the homeless.
6. Cut the grass, paint the shutters, or do some other service project for an elderly couple or person in your neighborhood.
7. Go hiking, swimming or something else fun and healthy.
8. Take your family out go-kart racing.
9. If expenses allow, spend a weekend rafting or canoeing.
10. If you're able, take each child on an overnight or weekend trip once or twice a year. Go see their favorite sports team out of town, or spend the night in a hotel, or go to a concert, or do something else fun one on one.

Identify Your Leadership Style

Have you ever considered your *style* of leadership?

At opposite ends of the leadership style spectrum are the *Control Freak* and the *Ostrich*. The Control Freak has to manage everything; while the Ostrich has his head buried and doesn't want to address anything. Most men fall somewhere in between, with a tendency to lean towards one end of the spectrum or the other. Or, for example, I've seen dads who are Control Freaks with their daughters and Ostriches with their sons. Or perhaps they are more controlling with one son and have their head in the sand with their other son. This isn't wrong in and of itself. You don't have to treat all your children the same. They are different. One child might police himself with television shows and turn off anything that isn't appropriate, while the other might watch whatever she can get away with. Even with twins, there can be significant differences. One might be mature and responsible, so you might get that child a phone. But if the other loses everything, he or she might not receive one. You have to parent to each kid as an individual.

What's important is to notice how you are parenting and to make sure you are parenting each child effectively. As with the adult twins who were raised in separate homes, we often end up doing either exactly what our dads did or the exact *opposite* of what our dads did. I have tried to figure out what my dad did right and imitate that—and to make sure I don't repeat his mistakes. Try to figure out what your style is and if you are leading your kids well.

1. Take an honest look at how you lead. Are you consistent in every area or do you vacillate?
2. Is your style fair and effective? Are you creating issues within your family by treating one person one way and another one some other way? Are you sensitive to differences in your children's personalities and adjusting your leadership style accordingly, while still remaining consistent in the big picture?
3. Trust your wife to be your critic. She can see things about your style that you can't. Consider her advice.

Take Care of Yourself

Being a leader means being a servant. However, it does not mean you should ignore your needs completely. Parenting requires giving of yourself in ways that push you to the edge of your comfort zone, but you will not be effective if you don't also find ways to take care of yourself. I believe that to be your best you need to take care of three areas of your life without fail: spirit, mind and body.

It's like a tripod—take away one leg and the whole thing falls down. Coach Teaff calls it the *three-legged stool*. Whatever analogy you use, all three elements are important to keeping you upright and completely healthy. Overdoing one leg does not compensate for neglecting the other.

To nurture your spiritual health, I encourage you to carve out time to get in the Word of God, pray, listen to some praise and worship music, and just be alone with God. It is also critical to your spiritual health, as well as that of your wife, to spend time praying with her. As the spiritual leader of your home, you will want to spend time teaching your kids about prayer, Bible reading and quiet time with the Lord. A key ingredient for me—and the one I have the most difficulty with!—is making time to be still and quiet so that I can listen for the voice of God.

Next, I believe you will be more effective if you develop a healthy mind. For me this includes reading, listening to podcasts of sermons and leadership messages like the ones Catalyst produces, and having some chill time. Because I live in the country, we have an ATV that I like to get on and just cruise around and enjoy nature. There is a creek I will go down to and skip rocks on; or else I just sit there and listen to the water run. There is a cliff overlooking the creek, and sometimes I go up there and lean back and take a little nap. It is lifegiving to clear your mind and just chill.

Finally, physical health is vital to achieving greatness in your home. I work out five or six days a week. I have found that the P90X program is a good fit for me. I can get a workout in at my house in about an hour. I also like to cycle. I have a couple of friends with whom I ride, and we push it pretty good for a bunch of old guys. I try to cycle two days a week and do P90X three or four days a week. I used to swim (when I lived in Dallas and had access to a good pool), and I loved mixing it up.

Find what works for you. Rather than making it a chore, I encourage you to make it a part of your lifestyle. If physical fitness hasn't been a part of your daily life for a while, don't feel like you have to get in shape in two weeks or even a month. Just begin to weave it into your lifestyle. *Ease* into it. Create short-term goals that lead toward a longer-term goal.

I discourage dieting. Nobody likes to diet and diets rarely work. Educate yourself about healthy eating and adjust your eating mentality if it needs it. My motto is that I eat to energize, not to get full. I love food, so this is something I have to keep a handle on. I am also a creature of habit. If I get on a roll of working out and eating right, I generally stay that way—until something knocks me off track. Usually it is an injury that keeps me from working out, and the eating often follows! I have also added in a day of fasting every week to aid in my spiritual health as well as my physical health.

Here are some simple steps to assist you as you pursue health of spirit, mind and body:

1. Make a commitment to spend time in the Word and in prayer; fellowship with other God-seeking men; participate in discipleship; find a church home; journal. And be still to hear the Lord.
2. Find ways to grow your critical thinking. Make a book list and carve out a few minutes every day to read. Listen to podcasts and make notes of great quotes or nuggets of wisdom. Find a "chill activity"—such as listening to music or hiking in the woods—that allows you to clear your mind.
3. Don't diet or try to get in shape in a month. Create a lifestyle of exercising and eating healthy.

Let Your Boys Be Boys

I know the Bible says that we were created in God's image, and I believe that in my heart. But I must confess, I wonder sometimes. Did God leave a wire loose on purpose, or not tighten a screw down all the way, when it comes to men? Maybe He knew we would need a "little bit of crazy" to accomplish His purpose in our lives. That's what I call the thing in men that doesn't always seem God-like. Most men are born with an innate desire to take risks and do dangerous stuff. We want to do things just to see if they can be done.

When it comes to bringing up boys, I encourage you to avoid the natural instinct to stifle that little bit of crazy. You probably acted on that little bit of crazy at times in your youth, and you know it caused you to do some dangerous stuff. I am not saying you should let your boys be reckless. Just make sure you don't squelch the very thing God put in them that would allow a young shepherd boy to come down from the mountains, look a giant in the eye, and say, "Who are you to come against the children of the most high God?"

You are the one who will grow that ability in your son if you nurture it properly. It is important that you get on the floor and wrestle with your boys, especially during their younger years. In their book *The Art of Roughhousing*, Anthony DeBenedet and Lawrence Cohen claim that roughhousing makes kids "smart, emotionally intelligent, lovable and likable, ethical, physically fit, and joyful."[1] Teach your sons how to change the oil, mow the yard and fix a flat. Do your own research on the benefits of letting your boys be boys. If your wife is overprotective, share the research with her and make your decisions about this as a team. Again, I am not condoning recklessness, but I do celebrate letting boys be boys.

Here are some ideas for how to implement the "let your boys be boys" approach:

1. Find ways to be physical with your boys: wrestle, play tackle football, or play them tough in a game of hoops.
2. Get your hands dirty with them by doing some good old-fashioned hard work. Teach them how to change the oil in a car or lawn mower. Build a piece of furniture or do some home repairs together. If you don't know how to do these things yourself, it's never too late to learn!
3. As they get older, read a book together like *Wild at Heart* or *Every Young Man's Battle*.

Note
1. Anthony T. DeBenedet, M.D., and Lawrence J. Cohen, Ph.D., *The Art of Roughhousing* (Philadelphia, PA: Quirk Books, 2010), p. 13.

Appendix B

What Every Team Member Should Know

What Every Dad Should Know

1. You should enjoy every phase of your kids' lives, because they won't last.
This was the best advice I received when my first son, Jake, was born. It came from my business partner, Craig Domann. It was meant for those early years, when there was feeding and changing and burping and holding. But as we both have seen our kids grow up, we've realized that it holds true for their whole lives.

2. You will mess things up.
Neither your marriage nor your kids came with instructions. You get to figure it out as you go. If you expect perfection, you are setting yourself up for failure.

3. Your kids will mess up.
Lead them to greatness and set high expectations, but understand that they are just as human as you are, and they will make mistakes.

4. Your wife will mess up.
I know this is getting repetitive, but you and I both need to be reminded. Just as we are selfish, prideful and sometimes unreasonable, so too are our wives. Extend the same grace and mercy to her that you want her to give you.

5. You should be the first to reconcile.

When you have a disagreement with your wife or your kids, you should go to them first to begin the healing process. This doesn't mean you have to admit to being wrong if you weren't, but you need to model a spirit of humility and openness. Listen to your child's version of why they want to do what they want to do (or did what they did). Don't give them the "because I said so" answer all the time. After listening to them, tell them why you feel differently and try to find a solution that makes sense to you both.

6. Your kids are always paying attention, even when it doesn't look like it.

You might think they are ignoring you, because they don't act like they are paying attention, but they are watching your every move. They are watching how you treat your wife, what you are watching on TV, how you talk to your friends, and how you prioritize your relationship with the Lord. They especially notice when your actions do not match your words.

7. Your wife is always paying attention, even when it doesn't look like it.

Your wife is also paying attention to how you treat her and talk about her. She will notice any inconsistencies. When she points them out, listen. Don't get angry or try to turn the tables by pointing out her issues. Invite her to be honest with you about these things and thank her for it.

8. Your wife and kids will tend to react to conflict the same way you do.

If you're an *exploder*, you will most likely create exploders. If you stuff your feelings, your wife and kids will probably begin to stuff theirs. And just as you have brought a conflict reaction style into your marriage (one that you learned growing up or that is based on your personality), so too has your wife. But you can lead her and your kids into a better way of resolving conflict. There is no excuse for abuse such as yelling or using harsh words. If this is your style, change yourself and then help your family to change.

9. You must "show" rather than "tell."

Don't just tell your family how to behave; set an example. I have never felt as convicted as I did when one of my boys yelled at the other one, and I stormed into their room and screamed at the top of my lungs, "We don't yell at our teammates when they do something we don't like!" My boys were quiet for a few seconds. Then they couldn't hold it in any longer, and they started laughing hysterically. I was still fuming and screamed again, "What is so funny?" Eli could barely get it out, but managed to explain that I had *yelled* at them not to yell. I had to laugh at myself, but inside I was crying. Enough said.

10. You can start now.

You may feel like it's too late, or that you've been messed up for too long. That is not true. Whatever changes need to be made in your home start *now*. If your kids are already out of the house, go to them and ask for their forgiveness. Share with them what you have learned so that they don't make the same mistakes you made.

What Every Child Should Know

1. Dad will mess up.

I remind my boys often that I am not perfect, but every mistake I make in parenting them is made in love. I am always doing what I think is going to be best for them in the long run; even if I am wrong, they need to remember that my mistake was made in love.

2. Dad will always love you.

Many kids fear that at some point, their parents will stop loving them. Make sure your kids know that will never happen. Again, lead them to greatness, but at the same time, make sure they know that no failure will ever stop you from loving them.

3. Jesus will always love you.

This sounds "churchy," but it's the only way I know to say it. Sound theology is scarce these days. This is something your kids need to be able to cling to when they are messing up.

4. God has a specific purpose for your life.
Each of us was fearfully and wonderfully made, as Psalm 139:14 affirms. All our days were written in God's book of life (see v. 16). Many people today lack a clear sense of purpose. Let your kids know they were made for good things.

5. You will mess up.
Your kids need to know you expect greatness, not perfection. Remember how I told Eli, when he was in the fifth grade, that he had to care about math? He didn't at the time. But when he was in the sixth grade, he was almost in tears over a bad math test grade. So we celebrated—not the bad grade, but the fact that he cared about it.

6. You are not what you do.
This is a life-long lesson, but one your kids can start learning early on. Don't go too gaga over a son being the starting QB for his junior high team, or your daughter being the head cheerleader, because one day they might not be those things anymore. When you heap too much praise on your children for their achievements, it's easy for them to think that your love and admiration were about their accomplishments. This can cause them to base their self-worth on what they do. I see it with many NFL players when they retire: They get depressed because their self-worth was tied up in being an NFL player, and now they don't have that identity to give them value.

7. We will always be on the same team.
It's okay to disagree and to have different viewpoints about certain topics; make sure your kids know that you will always be teammates, even when there is conflict. Many people think disagreement is bad. I think it is awesome, as long as team members stay engaged. If we were all robots who looked alike, acted alike and thought alike, life would be boring. Bill Parcells loved working with player personnel people who had their own opinions about players. He may not have agreed with them, but if someone could support his or her view, and was tough enough to stand up for it, that person had his respect.

8. I am for you.

When your kids' desires don't match up with your desires for them, they might feel like you're against them. Remind your children that you are on their side and you are for them.

9. I want the best for you.

I remind my boys all the time that I've been down the road they are on and have the benefit of experience. I remind them that I have been given the responsibility of protecting them, which comes ahead of my desire for them to have fun. In the end, I want what is best for them.

10. No mistake is so big you should stop trying.

Whether it is a child's grades, sports, music, friendships, walk with the Lord—or anything else they have made a mess of—nothing is too big a mess to stop trying.

What Every Wife Should Know

1. You think she is beautiful.

You cannot tell your wife *enough* how beautiful you think she is, inside and out.

2. You will never leave.

Your wife needs to know you are committed to her, especially if you have had a significant argument or disagreement.

3. You desire to be a great leader of your home and a great husband.

Let your wife know you take the responsibility God has given you, as a husband and a dad, seriously. She will appreciate your desire to pursue greatness, and she will be more supportive of your efforts.

4. You will mess up, but all your mistakes are made in love.

Just like with your kids, your marriage has no instruction manual! You desire greatness for your marriage, and even when you miss the mark, your mistakes will always be made in love.

5. You understand she will mess up.

Let your wife know that you don't expect her to be perfect. Let grace and mercy be the guide in dealing with each other's shortcomings.

6. You believe she comes first.

Many marriages revolve around the kids. This is a natural instinct, but your wife needs to know, and the kids need to know, *Mom comes first*. It's not a "who do you love most?" issue. Kids find security in knowing that Mom and Dad are committed to each other first. Kids are an integral part of the family, but not the center around which the universe spins!

7. You can be trusted.

Your wife needs to feel confident that when you say you are going to do something, you will do it. Give her every reason to trust you by being reliable, and by being open with her when you have difficulty following through on a promise.

8. You believe God is on the throne.

It is easy to get in the mindset that your home is your castle and therefore you are on the throne. Let your wife know that God is on the throne in your life. She will trust you more if He is.

9. You will be the spiritual leader of your home.

Many women have, by default, become the spiritual leaders of their homes. Make sure you assume the responsibility even if your wife wants to take on that role. She was not designed for it. That doesn't take anything away from who she is, or what her value is. In most cases, she will appreciate your stepping up to take leadership.

10. You and your wife are in it together.

At some point, you will face tough times—whether illness, financial struggles or other hardships. When my wife got sick, she felt guilty because she perceived that she was a burden on our home. Gradually, she began to isolate herself. I assured her that we were in the bunker together and that would never change. I reminded her that I *meant it* when I said my vows, and I knew she did too.

Acknowledgments

It is an amazing thing when you can marry your best friend. I would like to thank Layne, my wife, who is that and more. Your support and encouragement allowed me to complete this project. I am in awe of the complete person you are and how you inspire me to be greatness!

I appreciate how my incredible boys, Jake and Eli, challenge me every day and show me why it is so important for me to become greatness. You are both so awesome! God has *big* plans for you both, so fasten your seat belts and enjoy the ride!

This book would not exist without the assistance and influence of so many people in my life. It is impossible to mention everyone who has been an important part of the process. I must thank my mother, Suzanne Estle, and my stepfather, Bob Estle. You guys are amazing. Also, my sister, Julie Lowe, has always been such a loving sister, great friend and inspiration along with her husband, Charlie Lowe. You are both such a blessing. My in-laws, Grant and Donell Teaff, have inspired me beyond words. You have modeled what a marriage should look like and that is priceless.

I owe a great deal of gratitude to Jonathan Merritt for guiding me through the process. Without you I would just be one of those guys who wanted to write a book. You are *awesome*! I want to thank Ken Coleman for pointing me in the right direction and for always being so encouraging.

Thank you to my agent, Erik Wolgemuth, and all the great people at Wolgemuth & Associates. You took a chance on a first-time author and put your name and your reputation behind me. I know from experience that is no small step. Thank you.

I want to thank Margot Starbuck for all the efforts you put into this project. You saw the vision and became a part of it. Your editing skills put a much-needed shine on this material.

Many thanks to Craig Domann, his wife Teddi and their wonderful kids, for being great friends and great business partners for so many years. We have been through a lot and have lived to tell about it.

I'd like to thank my best friend, Michael Chenoweth. You hold me accountable and you support me unconditionally. I know you would do anything in the world for me, any day of the week, any time of the day. Thanks also to John Cruse, you are my brother!

I'd like to thank my pastors, Joe and Lori Champion at Celebration Church in Georgetown, Texas. You are inspiring and supportive in ways that have made connecting to my destiny possible. You are pastors in every sense of the word. You are a blessing to our whole family.

Thank you to all the awesome people at Gospel Light/Regal Books and Baker Publishing for the great ideas, design and hard work. You guys are consummate professionals and made the process easy and fun.

About the Author

J. Drew Pittman is a name partner for Domann and Pittman, one of America's premier sports management agencies. The firm has long been recognized as a leader in the industry, having had over one hundred players drafted in the National Football League (NFL) and one hundred more sign NFL contracts. Drew is a graduate of Southern Methodist University where he was a member of the nationally ranked soccer team. Drew resides in the Texas Hill Country north of Austin, Texas with his wife, Layne, and two sons, Jake and Eli.

Twitter: @DPFootballAgent

Facebook: First Team Dad

Instagram: dpfootballagent

YOU CAN BE A BETTER DAD... TODAY!

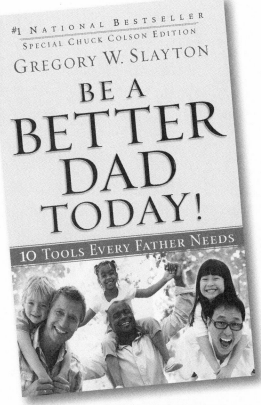

Be a Better Dad Today!
Gregory W. Slayton

Warmly endorsed by dozens of America's best-known and most-respected fathers, *Be a Better Dad Today!* lays out the "Ten Tools of Fatherhood"—tools to help every dad. This book is the product of Slayton's 30-year study of fatherhood on five different continents, his research into the subject, and his own experience raising four great kids with his wife of 25 years.

With humor, empathy, common sense and engaging stories, Slayton reveals proven, powerful techniques that will help dads fulfill their God-given responsibilities. Whether parenting younger or older kids, boys or girls, blended families or as a single dad (or even a father-to-be), you will find wise insights and practical, doable action steps for becoming the best dad you can be.

Available wherever books are sold!

Fight Like a Man

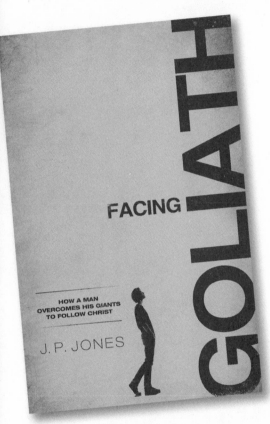

Facing Goliath
J. P. Jones

There is a giant standing between you and total victory in pursuit of Christ. What are you going to do about it? Whether it's the giant of doubt, fear, pride, lust or anger, there's only one way to defeat it: by fighting like the man God made you to be. *Facing Goliath* uncovers the kill zone of your enemies and arms you with the weapons you need to destroy them. Find out how to fight your Goliath with:

**The Truth of the Gospel
The Power of the Holy Spirit
The Authority of God's Word
The Provision of Prayer
The Armor of God**

Be like David, who ran full-throttle to attack Goliath, certain his God would give him victory against mind-blowing odds. Don't settle for defeat. Take your stand, because the battle belongs to the Lord.